Dear "Pat" —
Hope you find
this both enjoyable
& informative.
Take good care
of yourself & God bless.

Ray Berte

TO SPEAK AGAIN

"VICTORY OVER CANCER"

Raymond Berte, Ph.D.

PHILLIPS PUBLISHING CO.
P.O. BOX 439
AGAWAM. MA 01001

ISBN 0-941219-50-X

Table of Contents

Introduction

Ray Berte's story needs to be read by everyone confronting a major illness. Each of us is unique and the process of healing for each of us should proceed in an individual manner.

However, we can all learn from success. Ray's story allows us to see a pattern survivors can follow.

I have learned how important love, hope, and change are in the healing process. Ray lets us see how this can be incorporated into a life style. All of the changes Ray espouses may not be appropriate for everyone but they provide us with a blueprint for healing.

One has to remember that success is not an accident, it is hark work.

I know the role physicians may play to help in the process but the survivor takes responsibility and also participates.

We can all learn from Ray's story. We need not wait for an illness to occur. Hope and survival are not a matter of statistics. I hope health care providers will also understand that one can chase rainbows and catch them.

Bernard S. Siegel, M.D.
Author of *Love, Medicine, Miracles*

TO SPEAK AGAIN

FOREWORD

I do not want to add to cancer phobia. It is too rampant already, My intention is to give a more positive message to current and future cancer patients. Although this may sound contradictory to the above statement, I also want people to examine the question, "*Why not me?*" When cancer patients are diagnosed as such, one of the first things out of their mouths is "*Why me?*" What are you doing to protect yourselves, your families and friends, and others from getting cancer? The scientific community may one day come up with a cure for cancer; however, it makes more sense to me that *prevention* is "the" answer. Modern medicine has accomplished tremendous successes in treating many diseases and the advances in surgery have been nothing short of miraculous. On the other hand, on a scale of one to ten, I give mechanistic medicine a one in promoting health. I'm absolutely convinced that the holistic model is the way out. Yes, other people can and will help you. However, *you* must assume the major responsibility for maintaining your own health, and should you become ill, you must take responsibility for healing yourself, in partnership with the best medical advice you can get. Keep in mind: in the most essential ways, you are in charge of your life.

How I Felt

Part One

TREATMENT OF CHOICE

The feelings we have about any trauma are both unique and universal. Our unique feelings are often shaped and colored by memories, the distillation of our experiences. It is these vivid memories, described below, that surfaced and defined my personal response to the news that I had cancer. It is these affecting memories, some described below, that have served as grist for my personal growth.

Farmington, Connecticut, 1965

"OK, Ray, now vocalize nice and easy. Let it flow. Good breath control from the diaphragm and expanded back. Equipoise, equipoise. . . got it? And no bullshit white tenor, bow tie sound, I want it to come from your scrotum. We'll start with "La Donna E. Mobile," mid-range, and take it up step-by-step.

After about 20 minutes, with perspiration pouring out of my every pore, Bruce, my vocal coach, stopped me and said, "Guess what? That was your first high C. Not the greatest one I ever heard, but pretty damned good."

Talk about euphoria. . .I was flying. I was in ecstasy. From the time I was old enough to identify different singers and voices, I dreamed about one day making like Franco Corelli, my favorite tenor. With my crystal set, way back in the 1930's, I would listen to the Chicago Theatre of the Air, especially when the then young tenor Richard Tucker was going to sing. There's no sound in the world sweeter to my ears than a golden tenor hitting a high C.

During World War II most of my brothers were serving in the United States Army and I was a kid. My contribution to the war effort was to collect metal for recycling and to sing for servicemen of military installations and Veterans' Administration hospitals. When I was a high school student, I won a music scholarship to study voice. I sang in the Springfield Symphony chorus, many local groups, summer stock and again for the soldiers during the Korean War.

Seque. . .Redington Beach, Florida, June 1970

My five-year-old daughter, Jennifer, eight-year-old son, Keith, and I are seated at the dining table looking out the window at the Gulf of Mexico in Redington Beach, Florida, waiting for breakfast.

"Come on Mom, we want to get going. Bet we find all kinds of shells and sea urchins." That's the voice of Keith. He then pipes up with "Yeh, and you ought to give me more help with the rafts and fins and stuff. Dad and I do all the work; Mom and Jen just tag along."

After twelve years of Connecticut winters, my wife June and I bought this lovely little vacation home on the Gulf of Mexico, and June, an artist, turned it into an absolutely beautiful retreat that we could share with our children, Jennifer and Keith. It was a wonderful, restful place for June to escape the frantic pace of the commercial art world with its many deadlines.

At that time I was director of a compensatory education program, called Project Empathy, in the Farmington, Connecticut school system. My work, too, was very demanding and stressful. So, the Florida getaway was a most happy place for the whole family, especially when we explored the Gulf bottom, finding all kinds of aquatic life. When we returned to our Florida retreat home, after exploring the riches of the sea, we'd go through reference books to identify the different kinds of shells.

The first time we ever went exploring the sandbars off the beach at Fort DeSoto, Keith and I kept throwing small sand dollars back in the water and keeping the large ones. On our way back to Redington Beach, we stopped at a "tourist trap" in St. Petersburg Beach and saw a bin full of tiny sand dollars priced four for fifty cents. We all laughed when Keith reminded us we probably threw away two hundred dollars worth of sand dollars that day.

After supper and before sunset I loved to take one more refreshing swim. I particularly enjoyed swimming underwater and cutting to the surface with rivulets of water pouring down from my head and torso.

The whole family, including Jolie, our toy, white poodle, with a fondness for chasing fiddler crabs, would walk the beach enjoying the white sand, warm breezes, clean air and breathtakingly beautiful sunsets. Oh God, what a joy! All's right with the world.

Boston, Massachusetts, June 1973

As June and I entered Dr. Daniel Miller's examination room, I became excruciatingly aware that his very efficient and usually affable nurse avoided looking at me. She kept very "busy" with her back to me. Eventually she said, "The doctor will be with you momentarily," and sidled out the door, but not before I saw the tears rolling down her cheeks. A silent roar began to swell inside my head.

Dr. Daniel Miller, one of the best head and neck surgeons in the world, came into the examination room, took a deep breath, and said, "Ray, you have malignant throat cancer. I've agonized over how to best treat you: a partial or a total laryngectomy. I've checked with several of my colleagues, and we think the TREATMENT OF CHOICE is a total laryngectomy. It's not too bad. There are only two things you can't do following this surgical procedure. *"YOU CAN'T SING AND YOU CAN'T SWIM."*

The silent roar built up to a raging hurricane. No one could hear my silence. "You stupid son of a bitch! You have no idea what you're saying to me. Can't sing! Can't swim! That's worse than the death penalty!"

Know what's funny? On the way to Boston, from our Longmeadow, Massachusetts home, June and I were talking about several of our concerns, present and future; our children's education; should we buy that farm in the country; when will June be able to give up commercial art and concentrate on her painting. We heard the diagnosis and in that instant every problem I had in the world disappeared. Crazy! However, I have some new prob-lems to deal with don't I?

Let's go back to the beginning of this cancer journey. Project Empathy (a compensatory education program for disadvantage youngsters in the Farmington, Connecticut school system) had ended, and I joined the faculty at Springfield College in 1972. One of my oldest and best friends is Dr. Albert Alissi, faculty member at the University of Connecticut, Hartford School of Social Work. Al asked me to guest lecture one of his courses and I agreed. In the middle of lecturing, I began to salivate excessively and my voice went hoarse. After a couple weeks of raspiness, I went to an ear, nose and throat specialist in Springfield, Massachusetts, who, upon completion of his examination, said to me, "Well, at least it isn't cancer!"

"Cancer"---I never even gave it a thought. Me, get cancer...no way. Throat cancer...impossible. I never smoked and very rarely drank alcoholic beverages. Cancer...what a bad joke!

The doctor added, "It's some kind of virus that settled on your vocal chords. Take this medication and all should go well." The gravelly voice persisted. It was not painful, just a nuisance when I lectured. The most grief I experienced was in not being able to sing, even for my own enjoyment.

A few weeks alter my throat was examined again and the first doctor turned me over to one of his partners. The second doctor took one look and said you have to see Dr. Goldberg. The following week Dr. Sheldon Goldberg examined me and suggested a biopsy. Now I'm getting scared. Biopsies are only performed if there's concern about cancer.

I report to Mercy Hospital in Springfield and the biopsy comes back negative. No malignacny. Wow!!

However, the hoarseness obstinately held on and got progressively worse. Dr. Goldberg suggested I see Dr. Daniel Miller in Boston. "I studied under Dr. Miller and he's the best."

June and I trekked off to Boston and Dr. Miller suggested he do another biopsy. "There are lots of hidden parts of the throat that are very difficult to get at." So I was booked into the Ear, Nose, and Throat wing of Massachusetts General and had a second biopsy which turned out negative. "We'll keep a close watch on it and do a lot more testing."

During one of the battery of tests done on me at Massachusetts General, one of the residents sprayed my throat with an anesthesia to perform one of the examinations. The second he sprayed, my throat froze up and I began to choke. I was able to get out, "Oh oh, I'm in trouble. I can't breathe!" As I think back on the scene that followed, it was a tragic comedy. Everyone bailed out. Nurses, doctors, technicians all scattered in different directions while I sat in the examination room struggling to get a breath, breaking out in a cold sweat and thinking this is no way to go out. By the time the "pros" returned with emergency equipment, I had somehow cleared the blockage myself. After all the examinations were complete, I overheard one doctor saying to the other, "Boy, I sure learned something today." I said, "I'm sure you did and I paid for it," and left the room.

I was told to go home and relax for a couple of weeks while all the testing was finalized.

On my next trip to Boston, Dr. Miller gave me the news that I had malignant throat cancer. He thought that my best chances for survival rested on a total laryngectomy. His colleagues concurred, and I was told what the *treatment of choice was* to be. I meekly submitted to the verdict and surgery was scheduled for July 10, 1973.

Springfield, Massachusetts, July 4, 1973

I am number eleven of twelve children. When my family get together for a special occasion, it is a small army. My parents, brothers and sisters, their wives and husbands, nieces and nephews, cousins and grandchildren make for a large gathering of people. Add to the numbers the fact that my entire family is extremely animated. There's not an introvert in the group. Summer Sundays were spent playing volleyball, softball, swimming, horseshoe pitching, boccie, cards, listening to music, eating and drinking, etc. My brothers got special delight in ribbing one another during and after a ball game. "You couldn't hit a cow in the behind with a bull fiddle." "What were you throwing, watermelons?" On and on...

Fourth of July family picnic, the week before my throat surgery. The "conspiracy of silence," so well known by cancer patients, is extremely evident to one and all, especially me. Everyone's speaking in hushed tones. There's no spirit in the play. None of my brothers are teasing one another. Eventually we were all sitting around the dinner table in relative silence. Talk about the honesty and wisdom of a child. My daughter, Jennifer, eight-years-old at that time, said in a voice loud enough for everyone to hear, "You're not going to die, are you, Dad?"

My macho, stoic image was shattered. It felt like the weight of the world had been lifted from my shoulders. The unspeakable had been spoken. I took her in my arms and replied, "No, 'Nifer', not now. Someday your Dad will die, as we all will, but not now. Thank you for asking."

Boston, Massachusetts, July 9, 1973

There's a standing joke in my family that my brother-in-law, Joe DeCaro, gets lost every time he drives someplace he's not familiar with. He drove me to Boston the day before my surgery. I gave him directions to get out of Boston and on the Massachusetts Pike back to Springfield. Guess where he ended up? Yup...Cape Cod.

During pre-op preparation I was sitting in one of the examination rooms feeling lonely and frightened.

Without seeing him enter the room, I suddenly realized a dear friend, Dr. Leonard Plotkin, from Longmeadow, Massachusetts, was sitting next to me. He was my children's pediatrician. We didn't say much. It wasn't necessary. His presence spoke volumes. It was intimacy of the most beautiful nature. I'll never forget that loving scene. I took great strength from that man.

Flashback, 1930's and 1940's

As a very active, excitable youngster growing up in the North End of Springfield, I remember playing all the street games of that period, including "cops and robbers" and "cowboys and Indians."

My participation was great. However, all too often, these enjoyable moments turned into very upsetting experiences, some of the worst memories of my life. The neighborhood gang and I could be yelling and screaming, falling off "cliffs" with arrows in our backs, getting machine-gunned in a bank robbery, giving Tarzan yells swinging from tree tops and so on. Suddenly there could be heard the most ear-piercing, frightening whistle. My father came out of our house to quell the noise. When I heard that whistle my skin would crawl and my blood would freeze. My later professional training would identify this as a "conditioned response." Then came the worst part. Pa would berate me in front of the gang. "How come you're so noisy? You're too damned loud! You're the only one I can hear!" (It took me 30 years to realize I was the only one he was listening for.) At other times he would stand on the porch and when he caught my eye, he would grab his throat in a threatening gesture to communicate non-verbally, "Get home now, or I'll strangle you."

Massachusetts General, Boston, July 10, 1973

As I was being wheeled into the operating room I heard a very frightened little boy's voice deep inside me, "O.K., Dad?" "you won't have to listen to me anymore.

Some people believe in the theory of organs or targets of susceptibility. Elisabeth Kublier-Ross says there are no coincidences in life. I believe that is so. It is no coincidence that I got cancer in the throat. It is no coincidence *when* I got cancer in the throat. More about this later.

I woke in the post-op recovery room. It was a terrifying dream. I was in this large room with many beds positioned spoke-style with a nurse in the center of the wheel of patients so she could see us all. Most of the beds were occupied. I had catheters coming out of me; pressure bandages around my neck; feeling the desire to "get the hell out of here." It felt like the movie "Snake Pit," with patients wailing and crying. For the first time the realization that I couldn't talk struck me to the core of my being. My extreme fear caused a ton of weight on my chest; I couldn't breathe properly; my throat was full of liquids. "Call the nurse, you jerk. What's wrong with you? Call for help." How? There was no buzzer. There were lots of other patients and several of them were calling for assistance. How do I get the attention I desperately needed? I started to pound the slides of my bed with my fists. Bam, bam...one side then the other until the nurse came over and suctioned out the blood and fluids building up in my throat.

The next thing I remember was waking up in my room and seeing the beautiful face of my wife June looking down at me and administering her life-enhancing, therapeutic touches. They were so soothing I soon drifted back into sleep.

The next awakening was to a strange aberration. A person was standing over me, about nose-to-nose. When I opened my eyes fully, she said to me, "Get out of that bed, young man. I don't feel sorry for you, and neither should you." She turned out to be a speech therapist.

I'm sure her intentions were good. However, my professional training forces me to point out the fallacy of the approach she chose to speed up my recovery and shorten my mourning period. Also, this information is important to family members and professionals concerned with adventitiously disable people. Elisabeth Kubler-Ross enumerated the dynamic steps in the process of death and dying. She discovered these progressions when she was a general practitioner, dealing with patients who become disabled. One doesn't have to be told he is terminal to go through these dynamics. All that's required is for you to experience the loss of something/anything that you value greatly.

For the sake of brevity, I'll just list Kubler-Ross's dynamics and expound on the value of mourning:

(1) Denial. "Other people get cancer. Not me."
(2) Anger. I prefer the word "rage." I was absolutely enraged that my body was being violated; my body's integrity destroyed/demolished.
(3) Bargaining. Very irrational.
(4) Depression. Part of this step is called "preparatory grief." The patient is getting ready to mourn the loss and reach step five.
(5) Acceptance/Resolution. What has happened is a reality and now I must deal with it

effectively.

From the readings that I have done regarding this subject, and from my personal experience, it takes about eight to twelve weeks for most individuals to go through the above process and reach resolution. Some take years. Because most of us have been taught to avoid and deny negative emotions, we have a strong desire to short circuit others who are angry, sad, or depressed. Adventitiously disabled people must be permitted to go through the process outlined by Kubler-Ross and allowed to mourn their loss. The prognosis is usually poor for those who superficially examine their circumstances, deny their feelings and appear to bounce back without any difficulty. Sooner or later they'll crash.

For those individuals who don't reach the resolution stage in the rough parameters of eight to twelve weeks, the likelihood is that they'll stay stuck in depression. I suggest to any human-helping professional that she/he trust her/his intuition during this depressive period as to when it's time to get "tough" and confront the patient about getting on with living or allowing more time to mourn the loss.

Boston, July 11, 1973

Dr. Miller gave me the news that all went well with my surgery and that there was no lympahtic involvement. "I feel fairly certain we gòt it all." I was also told that my particular carcinoma is just about unheard of settling in the throat area. There are only about four cases in all the medical literature. Dr. Miller guessed that it was about twenty-five years since the last similar incident was recorded. I suggested my willingness to trade the notoriety for my normal vocal chords.

Hundreds of people sent me "get-well" messages and dozens came to visit during my hospital stay. I became irritable when my wife, family, and friends had to leave me. I remember one day in particular when some friends of mine left me and a few minutes later I was looking out my window at the Charles River and I recognized my friends walking along the river's pathway. I became very envious and angry with them. They could get up and leave the hospital, walk along the river, talk, whistle or sing! I had to stay behind in the hospital and never to able to talk, whistle or sing again. "To hell with you guys. I don't care if I ever see you again!"

Boston, Massachusetts, July 20, 1973

The bandages came off today. The thought is frightening. I'm shaking with fear. Dr. Miller says everything looks fine. After he leaves I go into the bathroom and see myself in the mirror. But, is that me? There's a hole in the center of my throat, my Adam's apple is gone, there are two long scars on either side of my neck. I can't stop trembling as I think, "What's June going to feel?" She has such a great eye for what's aesthetic. I'm repulsed by the way I look. In addition to surgery, I had lost forty pounds, which lowered my weight from 170 to 130. I'm ugly as sin.

This may sound too strong for some readers, but I really think I know what a woman feels like who experiences rape. My body's integrity was destroyed, violated, invaded.

Massachusetts Turnpike, July 24, 1973

When I was finally discharged from the hospital,

June and I stopped at a restaurant on the Massachusetts Turnpike to have some lunch. I ordered some clam chowder which was very hot. I automatically started to blow on it and began a long, silent laugh--which turned into a laughing/fit of crying. When June asked me what was going on, I wrote on my magic pad (remember as a child you had a wooden peg and pressure-sensitive plastic you wrote on then lifted the plastic sheet to make your marks disappear?), "I'm a neck breather now. I forgot about that. Do you think it would be improper if I held my spoon up to my stoma in order to blow on my chowder?" Then we both laughed.

When we arrived home I stood outside our house taking in the wonders of the area. The lyrics of the song "Welcome Home" from the musical *Fanny*--one of my all-time favorite shows--flooded my mind.

Welcome home says the street
As I hurry on my way,
Welcome home sings the gate like a song,
Welcome home says the door,
glad to feel your hand once more,
Now you're back where you belong,
Welcome home says the chair,
holding out its friendly arms,
Welcome home says the bed,
rest on me.
Now you're back where you should be,
close your eyes, close your eyes,
And the world will settle down to sighs
Welcome home says the lamp,
lighting up familiar things,
Look around at your friends good and true,
Get you cares all untied,
while you're warming up inside.

Welcome home to you.

Longmeadow, Massachusetts, August, 1973

While recuperating at home, June and I worked out a system of communication between us on the telephone. When we went to work, she'd telephone me and ask questions that could be answer by either "yes" or "no." I would tap the telephone's mouthpiece; one for "yes" and two for "no." It was a nice stopgap measure between the time my throat was healing and the start of speech therapy.

One day our eight-year-old daughter, Jennifer, went to a lake with some dear friends of ours. She was expecting to spend the weekend there. As it turned out, "Nifer" became mildly sick and stayed in the cottage while the others went off to swim. Gradually she became more nauseous and telephoned home for help. I was the only one at home and I was not expecting a call from June. The telephone rang and rang. I sensed an urgency in the ringing that finally prompted me to pickup the receiver. I could hear Jennifer saying, "Is that you, Dad? Daddy, I'm sick. Daddy, it hurts. I want to come home, Dad. Please!" I sat there feeling absolutely helpless. In my silence I was saying the unheard, "I hear you, sweetheart. You'll be O.K. Mom and Dad will come to you as fast as we can and ease the hurt." I never cried as hard as that in all my life. I hung up the telephone on her and jumped into my car; drove downtown to get June and then off to the lake to get "Nifer." I had to respond to that plea. The frustration of not being able to communicate properly in this instance was even more painful than in the post-op recovery room.

A number of laryngectomees came to visit me.

Their objective was to give support and information. However, I had an extremely negative reaction to the way they all sounded. If they used an electro-esophageal device, they sounded like mechanical robots. If they learned esophageal speech, they sounded even worse; gulping of air, stoma blasting; all kinds of extraneous noises. I thought to myself, "Hell, if that's what I'm going to sound like, I'd rather not even try." Professional rehabilitators refer to what I was experiencing as "expectation discrepancy." I didn't know at that time that it was possible for me to perfect and master esophageal speech way beyond what I was hearing.

Benevolently, my doctor chose to withhold the information from me regarding electroesophageal devices. I didn't know they existed. He thought that if I started using one I wouldn't be motivated to acquire the skill of esophageal speech. It really wasn't his decision to make, it was mine. Had I known about these prostheses from the beginning, it would have assuaged a lot of pain I felt, especially when it was my little girl hurting and reaching out for comfort.

Boston, Massachusetts, Fall, 1973

Checkup time in Boston. I had a shiny new Servox (electroesophageal device) hanging on a chord around my neck. My throat surgeon walked in, took one look at the Servox and said, "What's that?", even though he knew what it was. Answering him, I pressed the instrument to my neck and uttered my first words with my new voice; "You son of a bitch. Why did you choose not to tell me about these devices?"

Longmeadow, Massachusetts, Spring 1986

I didn't know it would happen. But reading and reflection about my experiences with cancer have made me a different person. In 1973 I had developed a new voice. Equally important, I have developed a new message...since I learned to speak again.

WHAT I HAVE LEARNED
READING AND REFLECTION

PART TWO

ADJUSTMENT TO DISABILITY

How do you survive a major physical calamity in your life?

Dr. Charlene DeLoach and Dr. Robert Greer wrote a wonderful book entitled *Adjustment of Severe Physical Disability*. In it they discuss a concept they describe as metamorphosis. This concept about disabled people proved very beneficial to me when I attempted to communicate to others that most disabled people have a wonderful adjustive ability inside themselves. When I say to people that I don't fell heroic and special in overcoming the difficulties of cancer, this is perceived as "modesty." This is not true. What I accomplished nearly every reader of this book can accomplish. The following excerpt from DeLoach and Greer's book says it better than I ever could:

> Metamorphosis is a term borrowed from the biological sciences and refers to a transformation of form. In nature, this is often a transformation from an unattractive creature (caterpillar) to a most attractive one (butterfly). Transposing this concept to the pro-cess of adjusting to physical disability--or "*stigma incorporation*," as we term it--makes the process a little less simple and obvious. The metamorphosis undergone by a person with a disability is *primarily on internal pro-cess*, involving a transformation in how the individual sees himself or herself. Only secondarily do those on the outside have a

chance to gain glimpses of this process through a changed presence on the part of the disabled individual. Such outward changes may be evidenced in a pleasant smile, a more assured posture, a brighter outlook for the future--and, in many cases, a sincere concern for others instead of, previously evidenced, a totally egocentric orientation.

In its biological framework, metamorphosis is a set, predetermined process. Some may not see this as analogous to the psychological processes involved in adjustment to disability, since such processes are not predetermined. However, the "blueprints" of nature are not always followed. Caterpillars do not always become butterflies and tadpoles are not always transformed to frogs! Though the process is completed more often than not, many external factors such as insecticides, predators, and the like must be considered. Analogous to this, there are external factors to be considered in adjustment to disability: what a teacher, counselor, or medical rehabilitator does or does not do can abet the metamorphosis of disabled persons, or thwart it.

The process of metamorphosis for the disabled individual is a gradual transformation of the individual's self-state. He or she has worked through the disabling myths to a certain degree, has learned to discriminate in evaluating the advice offered by professionals, and has begun to perceive assets, as well as liabilities, in a changed identity. As the disabled individual learns to focus upon and strengthen assets, she finds that liabilities can be safely relegated, most of the time, to the backstage areas of her world. Most of all, she discovers that life's agenda still beckons somewhere in the flux of places to go, people to meet, things to see or hear or buy, parties to plan, careers to develop-- there is an ever-evolving *raison d'etre*.

This process is, despite the media sterotype to the contrary, common to the great majority of those who grow up disabled or become disabled later in life. But, more importantly, its full fruition is not customarily realized in the form of a Franklin Roosevelt or a Helen Keller, Such truly remarkable persons are to be admired, but *should not be established as a yardstick* by which the achievements of other disabled persons are judged. Metamorphosis is a beautiful aspect of man's nature; and the most beautiful of its forms are the less dramatic, quiet resolutions of ordinary Jane or John Does who, finding themselves disabled, rise above all, or most, of the barriers to be discussed in this book to take their rightful places in life in the ordinary roles of wage earner, wife or husband, coworker, customer, citizen, and taxpayer. Only the few persons known to such Jane or John Does are aware of this process. No bands play, no movies are made with them in starring roles. They merely go about their daily routines as some of the marvelous monuments to the resilence of human nature.

We, the authors, sincerely hope that the reader, be you a professional in training, a practicing professional, a disabled individual, or a friends of the disabled, will acquire a fine tuned appreciation for the process of metamorphosis. Whether you take professional pride in observing it unfold in a client, personal pride in feeling to unfold in yourself, or an admiring pride in seeing it take place in a loved one, you will be in a better position to fully appreciate the traumas and triumphs involved.

BANNISTER SYNDROME

Deep inside yourself is a force that will help you overcome many disabilities. How powerful is that force? What are its limits? Do we have any influence on how far it takes us? Do you settle for less than you can get?

We need to push our limits. If you believe you can do it, you're on your way toward that realization.

Back in the 1950's there was a lot of talk about someone, sometime soon, running a mile in less than four minutes. No one had every done it before. A physician in England named Roger Bannister made it clear he thought he could do it, and he did. In the following couple of years, many men accomplished the feat of breaking this psychological barrier. If you believe you can do it, then you're on your way toward that realization.

One of my football coaches, a golden Greek named Nicholas Cosmos, used to say, "I don't' know anyone ever winning a fight who felt he was going to lose *before* entering the fight." I recalled those words when I was being urged to take chemotherapy and radiation which "might give me a couple more years to live." "Couple more years," hell; I was going for a win, and he's talking about giving me a few more months.

My singing teacher Bruce, who I mentioned earlier, used this approach in my vocal training. As a matter of act, every good teacher/coach I've ever met eschews giving their students/athletes a mind-set that builds in a limitation. Bruce wouldn't say we're now going for a high B flat. He just took me there.

A good track coach doesn't say to one of this charges, "The world record for this event is such and such." Rather, he says, "The last time you ran this event you did it in thirteen seconds. I'll bet this week you can cut your time down to twelve seconds. I'm sure you can achieve that time. You have the ability. Now go out and do it."

While I was recuperating from my esophageal operation, one of the members of the medical team asked me what I intended to do when I returned home. I wrote in my magic pad that I didn't understand the intent of his question. He said to me, "Obviously, you *can't* go back to teaching. *If* you're lucky enough to learn esophageal speech, it will take you two years, and even after that you can't talk more than ten to fifteen minutes at a time. It's too exhausting."

At the risk of sounding like a braggart, I feel the need to destroy a lot of myths and claptrap regarding laryngectomees, in particular, and cancer patients in general. I took me three months to master esophageal speech, and I've lectured as long as four hours with only a fifteen-minute break.

The Yale Medical School used to sponsor a Drug Dependence Institute where drug counselors could receive advanced training in this often frustrating profession. I was a drug counselor for three years and benefited from the tutelage I received at the Institute in New Haven, Connecticut. I was invited back for several years as a guest lecturer and had to "do my thing" in one day. I lectured from nine o'clock to noon and from one o'clock to four o'clock. Can't talk more than ten to fifteen minutes, eh? Hogwash!

Another doctor asked me what I did for recreational and physical activities. I told him I was always physically active, playing basketball, football, tennis, swimming, etc. As a youngster growing up I "lived" in the Springfield Boys' Club. Along with most of the kids growing up in the North End, I was expected to master all kinds of physical activity from tumbling and gymnastics to ping-pong and pocket pool. The physician proceeded to ask me if I ever lifted weights. That was one activity I had never tried. His response was, "Good. You *can't* lift weights because when you raise them over your head the clavicles (i.e., collarbones) come together and pinch closed your stoma (i.e., the surgical opening in my throat area through which I breathe)." I thought about this for a few moments and envisioned the burlesque scene just described. I asked myself how long does a weight lifter hold the weights overhead? Five minutes? Three? Or merely seconds? Guess what was one of the first activities I engaged in after leaving the hospital? Right on!

The power of suggestion and the colossal effect of words are more than flesh and blood can bear. All human-helping professionals must develop an appreciation of the hypnotic effects their words have on many of their patients/clients. Of what benefit is it to patients to hear negative qualifiers like: Don't, Can't, If, Maybe, Must Not, *ad nauseam*. To ameliorate pain and suffering, we want to transmute negativity into the positive energy of "live" messages. Change "*If* you're lucky" to "*when* you master esophageal speech."

I appreciate the fact that there are certain parameters necessitated by surgery and medication. However, more often than not, I think we need to push our limits. With the doctor's permission, I inflame cancer patients with the vision that they are capable of doing much more for themselves than they think. With judicious use, figuratively speaking, I encourage women with mastectomies to forget "tiptoeing up the door with their fingers." I want them to grab the top of the door and hang from there.

Live and Get-Lost Messages

How do we nurture the "good stuff" in us and in others, enhancing our chance to transform ourselves?

Several psychotherapists I've worked with professionally use colloquial expression to demonstrate the kinds of messages we tend to give to one another. Some of these messages are helpful; some, destructive. At the two extremes are "live" and "get-lost" messages.

In my counselling practice, "I've heard these "get-lost" utterances:
--Wish you had never been born.
--If I never see you again it'll be too soon.
--Why don't you go play in traffic.
--Get out of the kitchen, etc.
--What can you expect at your age? You know
    you're not a teenager anymore.
--Do as I say. Don't make waves.

Also, in my counselling practice, I've heard these "live" messages:
--We're so lucky to have you around.
--We're so lucky you were born to us.
--You know you're loved.
--You *can* do it.
--Have a nice forever.
--Please drive carefully.
--You count, too, etc.

One of the nicest therapeutic things we can do for one another is to give "live" messages. It doesn't take much energy to do so, and giving "live" messages is so constructive.

In the thirty-three years June and I have been

married, we have had twenty "unwanted" children living with us for different periods of time. Consider this: Fifty percent of all births in the United States are unwanted. It will take a lot of "live" messages to offset the poor self-esteem of these unwanted children.

Pronouncements of doom don't help anyone. "You may have six months, one year," or whatever time, is a terrible statement. The patient might "buy" into it. "If you opt for this treatment, we'll probably give you a couple of years." Nuts!

The day that I was diagnosed as terminal I stopped to see my friend Alex Rossman, a certified genius and a most knowledgeable nutritionist. I was in a deep depression and expected the bad news to devastate Alex. When I said I probably had six to eighteen months to live, his reply was a glorious, life-enhancing message: "Six months--great! That gives us plenty of time to work it out." Can you imagine how uplifting that was for me? It was magnificent.

Another example of physical and emotional healing took place the time I was thinking of leaving the United States to try some nontraditional cancer treatment methods. My dear friend Dr. Angelo Bilionis gave me his personal check--blank at the time--and said, "Whatever you think you'll need, go for it." Beyond the obvious material offering, I could feel his healing energy. I repeat, "get-lost" messages are harmful and "live" messages have a beneficent effect.

Another precious friend, John Miller, said to me during my stay in Boston, "you're on a tough road, old friend, but somehow, some way, knowing you as I do, you'll make it."

A male nurse, whose name I don't even know, contributed enormously to relieving my pain and adding to my life-energy source. This unknown "angel of mercy" came on duty at Massachusetts General for the night shift, my most painful, helpless-feeling periods happening in the wee hours of the morning. He would come into my room several times every night to check on me. "How're you feeling, Ray? You're looking better all the time. I don't know you personally, but somehow I get the feeling you'll be just great after this is over." He would always touch me, not in the pursuit of his job responsibilities, but in a humanistic, therapeutic way that I've never experience before or since. God bless you, my unnamed, unknown nurse.

Following several cancer outbreaks, I stopped by one of my favorite clothing stores one day and saw a jacket that I liked very much. I enjoy nice clothes and wanted to purchase the garment. I thought to myself, "What a waste" and left the store without the jacket. I drove about a mile, did a U-turn, and went back to buy the jacket. "Come on Ray, you give "live" messages to those you love, surely you can give them to yourself." (By the way, I've worn out that jacket.)

My wife and I planned on buying a farm in the beautiful town of Suffield, Connecticut, when I was diagnosed as terminal. At first I thought: that's the end of our beautiful dream to get back to nature. June and I discussed this at length and made this watershed decision: let's continue to plan our lives expecting to live a hundred years. Since I reached that conclusion, I've shared it with many other cancer patients. "Continue to live your lives with the expectation in mind that you'll reach 100 years old.

All of my six brothers have great affection for their families, but like our father, we have this macho business of not expressing verbally to one another that we truly feel this way. Symbolically and nonverbally, they'll communicate their love. At one time, while I was at a cancer treatment clinic thousands of miles from home, I received a telephone call from my brother Fred. He wanted to know how I was feeling and what my cancer treatment program was like, etc. Finally, for the first time ever I heard words of affection spoken by one of my brothers. He said, "You know, kid brother, I love you very much. You are much-loved by so many people. We all miss you." Wow!

The first lecture I gave upon my return to work at Springfield College was a peak experience. I was using on electroesophageal device then, and I was fearful about my ability to communicate. How was I coming across? Are they getting it? What did I sound like to my students? Were they paying more attention to how strange I sounded, or were they hearing what I wanted to share with them? I'm sure my nervousness was noticed by most of the class, and I kept asking them for reassurance. The class turned into a revival meeting. One by one, the students started yelling out to me: "Keep it coming, Prof." "You sound good to me, Doc." "I hear you loud and clear, Ray." The air was electric, and emotions were high. The room was filled with love. When I completed my lecture and dismissed the class, the students rose as one and gave me a standing ovation. They breathed new life into my disabled body.

Elisabeth Kubler-Ross says the first significant lesson in her life was that it take *one human being who really cares* to make a difference between life and death. To help instill more humanity in a world full of inhumanity, it would be so wonderful if all of us would give "live" messages without reservations.

Really, dear reader, it takes very little effort to make a big difference in someone's life.

Too many human-helping professionals are callous, and sometimes downright stupid, in the negative suggestions they communicate in a blase manner. Moreover, mechanistic medicine places patient and physician in environments often not conducive to sustained healing.

We are all somehow connected. I believe there is a universal life energy which sustains our existence. If one person's battery is low, another can help charge it by saying and/or doing something positive. Cancer patients are not slabs of meat, devoid of spirit, only to be poked and probed. Have faith. Give hope. That's love.

Under certain circumstances we have all experienced our capacity to help others heal themselves: we have all eased somebody's distress. We know, at some level of consciousness, the power in all of us to make "it" better for ourselves and for others. We really need to enhance this God-given ability to give "live" messages.

What I'm about to say sounds so self-evident some readers may think I'm simple. "You have to breathe in order to live." Cut off breath, and you rob life at once. There are degrees of breathing; therefore, degrees of feeling alive.

As we all know, our breathing is affected by events in our lives--fear, shock, laughter, tears, etc. Some things will help stimulate our breathing, and others will depress our breathing. We need to breathe deeply to be fully alert and alive. Through caring, touching, and what we say and do, we can affect our own breathing and the breathing of others. "Live" messages help achieve this end.

Most of our cures are really the simplest.

Remember when Mom kissed your boo-boo when you were in tears because of a cut finger, and you went away laughing? How about the time Dad held you in his arms because you needed comfort and protection? They were just being lovingly human. They were at your service, and when the need arose, they responded appropriately.

At the risk of sounding maudlin, this kind of attention may be the basis of all true healing. Someone loves you enough in a selfless way to respond to your needs. They give "live" messages. Is there a better medicine? We all need this. For all of us are patients at different times.

RESISTANCE TO CHANGE

What is the greatest obstacle to seeing that transformations take place in you?

Sociologists refer to it as "cultural lag," which means that society's recognition of the need to respond to a crisis is lagging. In other words, the need precedes the culture's awareness of the need to be met. (Does this make sense?) We are "dragging our feet," so to speak. We seem to have this built-in resistance to new ideas and to change.

We are taught certain things and incorporate them into our psyche, our belief systems. Someone suggests there may be other alternatives, other beliefs and values, and when we run them through our old beliefs and see they do not match we discount the new. Your mind doesn't want you to questions your belief system.

Please don't wait for some serious, precipitous event like contracting cancer to consider some changes in your behaviors and beliefs. Keep an open mind. Consider the possible benefits and dangers of alternatives you are not aware of, or refuse to contemplate.

The diagnosis of cancer can be devastating, enough to break the sturdiest spirit. Most people equate cancer with death. This is not so. It doesn't have to be so.

There is always a considerable time lag between the scientific validation of a medical treatment and its acceptance by the general public--by state legislature--by federal agencies.

Bias against nutritional procedures appears to me

to be especially deep rooted, particularly in the case of cancer treatment and prevention.

People in general are automatically suspicious of anything that threatens the status quo. This is a human tendency. Most people are too conservative and basically negative. I anticipate this resistance anytime someone asks me about holistic medicine and ancillary treatments. "Oh, no." "You can't do that." "My doctor wouldn't approve," etc.

It appears to me that physicians in particular almost instinctively react with aversion anytime I mention vitamins and nutrition. However, I must say more and more physicians--especially the ones I know--realize the significance that good nutrition will increase their competence in helping cure patients.

Historically, medicine's resistance to new ideas comes from a desire to protect the patient. That is understandable and desirable. However, this conservatism goes too far. As with any virtue that's carried to an extreme, the virtue becomes a fault. I wish more doctors would apply skepticism to the propaganda proliferated by the drug industry. Many of the drug addicts I've counselled know more about the effects and negative side effects of certain drugs than a number of physicians I know on a social basis.

"Change" means letting go of the past and risking something new. Every stage in human development involves "letting go" in order to take advantage of the "new."

By now you must realize the critical importance I place on using your own body's resources to fight cancer, and any other disease. Others have used the term "enlist your internal doctor" to keep you well and help cure your ills. By all means find good doctors you have confidence in to aid you when outside help is needed. You must avail yourself of their expertise. However, don't become over-reliant on medical technology. You have to heal yourself. Motivate yourself with a religious fervor and belief in inner strength. I believe that God gave all of us that power.

I was raised with the belief that older people and authority figures knew what was best for me. "Listen to the authority figure and follow instructions without question and to the letter."

When my mother was eighty-four years old, and showing some signs of senility, I suggested some vitamin therapy might be appropriate. Her response to me was, "Raymond, I can't do that unless my doctor tells me to do so."

As an aside to the above:" My mother had soup almost every day for lunch. Frequently I would stop by the house at lunch time and without her realizing it I would slip some powdered niacin into her soup, which gives an oxygen release into the blood, which in turn meant more oxygen reaching her brain. She would eventually sit upright, wide eyed with wonder and say, "Raymond, I feel better." I never told her what I was doing to her soup.

I'm not sure of the source, but think it was Thomas Aquinas who said there are no miracles. Miracles are simply undiscovered knowledge, or words to that effect. Think about that for a minute and see the great wisdom in it. *Miracles are simply undiscovered knowledge*. Years ago who would have believed you could have some control over your heartbeat, skin temperature, blood pressure, and respiration? All kinds of recent experiments in biofeedback have indeed revealed we can mentally preside over a wide variety of bodily functions, previously considered involuntary.

Cancer patients must be aggressive in gaining knowledge. In my opinion, the medical/scientific fraternity in the United States maintains a cultural arrogance that kind of brown outs/messes up achievements in other countries. On the flip side of that coin we take credit for ideas based on research findings that have been practiced for centuries in other cultures. We have much to learn.

The history of mankind is filled with controversies in just about every subject you can list, from science and medicine to religion and art; from politics and sports to child-rearing practices and educational theories. "Today's radicalism becomes tomorrow's orthodoxy." Claudius Galenus (130-200 A.D.) was hassled all his life because he believed that blood, not spirits, flowed through our arteries.

Hundreds of years ago trephining (drilling holes in the skull in order to let evil spirits out) was common medical practice, along with bleeding. Pasteur was laughed at for talking about germs, bacteria, and disease. Dr. Boylston in 1721 was nearly put to death for trying vaccinations against smallpox. American physicians wanted laws passed that would imprison both the doctor (administering) and patients (submitting) to vaccinations. Austrian physician Dr. Semmelweis in 1861 was vilified by his professional peers for suggesting they wash their hands before helping women deliver their babies. Who would have suggested that someday we would land human beings on the moon? Or give organ transplants? Or conceive of bioengineering? Can we make a wheelchair that will climb stairs? Wow!

Can you imagine the courage it took for Professor Richard Ahreus, back in 1970, at the University of Maryland School of Nutrition, to suggest more nutrition courses for students in the School of Medicine?

He was shot down, of course. "What are your proposing Professor Ahreus? Nutrition courses for our overcrowded medical schedules? Our students need more time and information about more and more drugs." What nonsense.

My point in all of this is the resistance to change not to belittle the medical profession. For superpersonal reasons I want--and expect--to be alive in the year 2000 in order to see what has evolved into traditional cancer treatment.

If you are sick, by all means go to a doctor quickly. Don't be foolhardy and think you can treat yourself, if you are really sick. See your doctor first and enlist proper nutrition to help you fight off the illness.

Dr. John Diamond points out to us another example of resistance to change when he lectures on the thymus gland. Up until fairly recent times the thymus was frequently surgically removed or irradiated from children on the false assumption this would reduce illness.

Evidence accumulated during the last twenty-five years or so on the role of the thymus in immunology is so astounding that Dr. Diamond believes there may be some unconscious factor at work denying the recognition of the invaluable contributions of this gland. He often hears, "everyone knows that the thymus gland has no function in adult life."

Transitions/changes in all our lives are characterized by conflict and confusion. The old ways are familiar territory. We've learned how to adapt to them, New ways, new ideas, new ways of perceiving, thinking, feeling cause resistance.

I use a technique (often in counselling) where I draw a path that twists and turns, loops, detours, eludes, sidesteps, etc., which may or may not reach a destination. My illustration looks like a mass of broken, twisted spaghetti. This sketch represents the road travelled by my client to reach a destination, a conclusion, solution, or what have you. Then I draw a straight line between two points to demonstrate a new road that could be taken. Guess which route the client takes? You're right..it's well-known, as painful as it is.

Every day of your life represents an opportunity for a new beginning. I strongly suggest you expand your consciousness and extend your living spaces. Risk new behaviors, new ideas and methods.

Webster's Dictionary in 1933 defined uranium as "a useless metal." Sure wish I owned a pile of that useless stuff. I'd be a wealthy man.

Ashley Montague said, "...most ignorance is voluntary, and there is not health in that, only narrowness, impoverishment of spirit, and bigotry."

Arthur C. Clark's famous "Third Law' states: "Any sufficiently advanced technology is indistinguishable from magic."

People often wait until they are in the terminal phase of cancer before considering adjunctive, alternative healing therapies which also fail as did the traditional ones. Then the nontraditional therapy gets ridiculed and thrown out as useless. Do not wait that long, dear readers. Get information; explore other health-promoting techniques. Watch out for the "quack" and the "quick fix artists."

New territory being explored in any field is bound to be criticized--often unreasonably so and by self-serving opposition. Advances often face intense opposition by close-minded individuals. Why should there be such resistance? Could part of the answer be that you may be wrong; your beliefs are really ill founded?

Thomas Edison once said, "Until man duplicates a blade of grass, nature can laugh at his so-called scientific knowledge. Remedies from chemicals will never stand infavorable comparison with the products of nature--the living cell of the plants, the final result of the rays of the sun, the mother of all life."

Back in the 1950's, when I was an undergraduate student in college taking a course in gerontology, I read about a Professor Anna Aslan, at some geriatric institute in Hungary, who was doing some fascinating experiments in the treatment of senility. Some of her results were miraculous. Professor Aslon injected these old people with some animal extract, (I don't know what it was) and some of them gained weight, regained their hair color, gave up their depressions, conversed and interacted more with other people, and were more physically active. Professor Aslan seemed to turn back the clock for these old people.

She was scoffed at, and her therapy treatments were not adopted by other professionals. What astonished me were the reasons given for the oppositions: "Her treatment is too simple. It couldn't possibly work clinically." "It works for her because of her personability (i.e., "bedside manner") and rehabilitation methods, "She gives vitamins and minerals."

Her detractors couldn't explain her successes so her work must be fraudulent. Crazy!

Is there a more frightening/forbidden word in the English language then "cancer?" Many people who do horoscopes refer to those born under the cancer sign as "Moon Children." When a member of a family is known to have cancer, relatives will seldom discuss the illness openly, as if actually to name the disease would ensure the death of the sufferer. Once cancer is diagnosed, the rest of the family behaves as if the sufferer is already dead, and most people still think of the disease as being nearly always fatal. Nuts! We have to stop equating cancer with death. We must stop conjuring up these terrifying images. We must learn to discuss the illness openly and honestly.

Fear of the disease is so great that many women finding a lump in their breast delay going to the doctor, terrified that he/she may confirm they have cancer. Men with similar lumps on their testes follow the same self-destructive route.

If the armor of fear can be penetrated enough to ensure that people seek early medical treatment, the prognosis for recovery is much better.

I'm fearful of the scientific community. They all too often think they know *the* answer to life and living. They don't. The artists do--like playwrights, poets, musicians, authors--are more trustworthy, in my opinion.

Readings in the popular press and scientific journals should arouse much concern in all of us. I'm referring to subjects like "embryo technology," exotic techniques to produce "super babies," the possibilities of producing children, without the male contribution to fertilization, and so on. Does the scientific community think that we the people are incapable of change and therefore must be changed by them in order to survive?

NO COINCIDENCES IN LIFE

When cancer patients are diagnosed as such, one of the first things out of their mouths is "Why me?"

One time my son Keith was excited by the possibility of winning first prize in an art contest in school. I think he was in the second or third grade. The contest was to see who could design and make the most interesting bookmark. The first prize was a book about dinosaurs and in the first grade Keith had expressed an interest in becoming a paleontologist. When I asked him what a paleontologist does, he replied, "That's a scientist who studies fossils and bones in the 21st century." In any case, he had his heart set on winning that most cherished book and June volunteered to help him. Keith told her that her helping him wouldn't be fair because she's a professional artist and, "Besides, Mom, I have to do this myself."

When the winners were announced, Keith was not among them. He was disappointed but accepted the loss without any fuss, until the teacher said to him, "Keith, your bookmark was really the best, but of course we know your mother helped you." He was crushed. His honesty was denied and he was mortified. He came home and we had a family conference. This was a teachable moment. June and I communicated to Keith and Jennifer both that this is not a just world. There are no guarantees in this life, and we all, sooner or later, learn the painful lesson: life isn't fair. June went on to visit the teacher the next day to fill in the missing parts and enlighten her about the potential destructiveness of what she said.

This account of my son's growth experience is an introduction to the concept that needs to be understood by cancer patients, their kin, and people in general.

Most cultures believe in a "just world" theory, also called the "myth of sin." Somehow virtue and reward go hand-in-hand. On the other side of that coin, evil and punishment/suffering go together. In our minds we want to make this fit: If the result of something is bad, then the cause must have been bad. To the ancient Hebrews, illness and physical defect marked the person as a sinner. The Trobriand Islanders believed that any affliction of a tribe member could be blamed on an enemy, thought to have caused the ill fortune through some kind of sorcery. We want to believe that suffering is reserved as a punishment for evil. Our sense of justice requires this. We deserve what we get.

Human nature forces us to search for reasons and find answers. We need to know. When we don't have the answers, we try to fill in the missing parts and make sense out of mysteries. The belief that suffering is caused by something evil, something sinful, is easy to accept.

I was taught as a child by my family that if you do something bad, you will be punished by God. My childhood perception of what my church taught about God was the same. One day I skipped school with a friend, and as we walked along the sidewalk, I was saying to him, "You know we are going to be roughed-up by god for this," and I walked into a street lamp pole and hurt myself pretty badly. Talk about reinforcing a belief!

After the third time I was diagnosed with cancer I went out and sat in my car. I was scared and wondered and grew steadily more angry until I shouted with all the gusto I could manage, not having vocal chords, "Hey, Big Guy up there, what the hell did I do. Was I so terrible? When? I've had enough of this! Spread some around to those sons-of-bitches who are the destroyers of the world. Can't you see that I love people? I wouldn't knowingly hurt anyone!"

When Keith was twelve years old his nose started to bleed for some unexplained reason. We tended to it and sent him off to bed. About two o'clock in the morning he awakened June and me with blood all over him and with his bed sheets bathed in blood. We rushed to the hospital emergency room, and the resident doctor couldn't get the bleeding to stop. An ear-nose-throat specialist was called in and performed surgery. It didn't work. Keith was in and out of surgery eight times in the next six days. Finally, with police escort, we rushed him to Massachusetts General Hospital in Boston. We were met at the door by my cancer surgeon, who took one look at Keith and said, "Prepare him for immediate surgery." I came unglued. I dealt so much better with my own pain. I could accept that. But my kid. Oh, God! What now? Could my son possibly be paying the price for someone else's infraction?

I don't know the answer. I'm not even sure of what questions to ask. Following any experience each of us has to arrive at some conclusions, make some decisions. My beliefs are difficult to explain with any great clarity. With courage, I'll continue, however, to describe how I sense things.

I attended a workshop featuring Elisabeth Kubler-Ross, and I heard here say, "There are no coincidences in life." I interpret that statement to mean there is a design, some connection, some purpose, some meaning to everything that happens. However, I don't believe that everything that happens to us is the predestined will of God. I would find it intolerable and unacceptable to believe in a God that would will the barbarous happenings we confront every day in the news media and in our personal lives. The contradiction which I still have to resolve is that I think there is a purpose, a greater design to my getting cancer. I'm not sure what it is. I can only come up with conjectures at this time.

Let's return to my son during the nose-bleeding trauma. The summer of this incident he grew so fast and tall that his body couldn't meet the accelerated growth requirements, and a blood vessel burst in the roof of his mouth. After having it attended to surgically, our friend Alex Rossmann suggested getting some liquid calcium and magnesium into Keith to strengthen his bones and blood vessels, which worked wonders. The week after Keith got out of the hospital he went and played soccer at school obviously without his parents' permission or knowledge. He took a "shot" right on the nose, and it didn't every bleed.

I learned a most important lesson from the nose-bleeding experience. After Keith's repeated trips to the operating room, I become aware of family and friends saying things like, "Boy, that kid is tough," "He never cries," "What a courageous boy," "He's so strong for one so young," and other similar remarks. The destructiveness of what was being communicated struck me like a thunderbolt. I literally quivered. It was an Epiphany moment. People were, unintentionally, of course, reinforcing what ought not to be reinforced. But we live in a culture that drives us to *be strong* to the great detriment of persons who can only be human with human frailties.

My son was expected to be strong, be macho, deny his pain and feelings, and only suffer internally. CRAZY! Just before Keith was wheeled into the last operation I picked him up in my arms, with tears streaming down my face and apologized for the insensitivity of us adults. "It's really O.K., son, if you get angry, if you want to cry and shout at the hurt and injustice of all this."

Later on we talked about my belief that it takes strength to admit to weakness. It takes courage to ask for help. The "trip" being laid on ny son was the same one "zapped" into me: Deny your feelings! Be a man! Be strong!

One of my favorite songs comes from the most touching scene in any Broadway musical--when Marius, the young son, sings to his father in the musical *Fanny*:

I like you,
Like you very much,
More than I could ever show.
I like you; it's not much to say,
But I need to tell you so.
Sometimes you wait to say things;
you wait too late.
Days that once seemed so slow,
how fast they go.
Words spoken,never mean to much.
Still, I just want you to know:
I like you.

Could this valuable lesson be a coincidence? I think not. Am I expected to share this information with others? I think so. Why do people at a particular point in their life contract cancer in a particular organ. Coincidence...no way!

Thomas Jefferson and John Adams both died on

July 4, fifty years after the signing of the Declaration of Independence. David Phillips of the State University of New York at Stony Brook recalls Jefferson's last words, as quoted by his physician. The doctor described the end. "About seven o'clock the evening of July 3 I was at Jefferson's bedside when he exclaimed, "Oh, Doctor, are your still there? It is the fourth? To which I replied, "It soon will be." These were the last words I heard him utter."

One of my students was born the same day her brother died. Coincidence? No way. Shortly before the opening of every musical I appeared in I developed either a cold or laryngitis, or a sore throat, or I came down with some kind of virus, resulting in a temperature and nausea. Coincidence? Could be getting ill allow me to rationalize a less than perfect performance? After all, I could have been better if I weren't sick.

When I was a kid I remember reading an account of Eddie Rickenbacker, the great pilot, lost at sea with several other crew members. I think they were either downed by a German pilot or their airplane had mechanical failure. In any case, after being afloat in the life raft for days and weeks, they ran out of food and water and were on the brink of death. Some drinking water was trapped in a sudden rainfall, and then a strange thing happened. A sea gull flew down and landed right on Rickenbacker's head. The bird was captured and eaten and provided enough nourishment until a rescue ship came along soon afterward. Coincidence?

In all our lives we experience twists and turns and forks in the road. We have choices to make. We attempt to make sense out of those choices. Things, events, experiences don't just happen in isolation.

There is some connection. I have to believe that. There is some greater purpose, some master design unfolding.

When I was in high school I was faced with a big decision. I was given free voice lessons, won a music scholarship to college, and considered making a professional career of singing. I was singing in the Springfield Symphony Chorus, starring in high school musicals, and was part of an entertainment troupe that went to Veterans Hospitals, and the like. The director of the entertainment troupe was known, by all who worked with him, to open the show with this second best act and close with his best. Usually it would come down to a choice between an Irish tenor and me (a spinto tenor, which is a darker, more dramatic sound than the lyric, light-sounding Irish tenor). Sometimes the director would make his choice depending on the audience. Other times he would listen to us warming up (vocalizing) before the performance and then decide who sounded better to him. One night the director said, "Patrick you open tonight, and Ray will close." Patrick got angry and said, "No, let Ray open and I'll close." I argued some but capitulated to Patrick's fury. My rationalization for giving in was, "Well, Pat, if it's so important to you, go ahead and close. I'll open."

Later on, I thought very seriously about the incident. I concluded "If it wasn't equally, or more, important to me than to Pat making a profession of singing was not my best career choice." Just think if I had gone into singing and then contracted throat cancer. Coincidence?

When I went to the Sidney Farber Cancer Clinic in Boston for some further cancer tests, the physician who examined me wrote to my oncologist,

"This guy's chasing rainbow," About a year later, June and I visited a lovely private school and camp in Vermont. We were invited to have lunch with the youngsters enrolled there, and seated at our table were two beautiful boys who spoke with foreign accents. They were introduced only by first names. After lunch we were told that they were the sons of the famous Russian author Solzhenitsyn. The camp and school director, who also had cancer, told me about Solzhenitsyn's own cancer battle and a book Solzhenitsyn wrote called *Cancer Ward*. Solzheitsyn wrote about the rainbow colored butterfly was a symbol of life. Was I chasing rainbows? You're damned right I was!

From my psychological training I learned that the unconscious is the same the world over and that many symbols are the same cross-culturally and over the generations.

Studies have been done regarding organs as targets of susceptibility. I repeat, it's not a coincidence where cancer is located. It's not a coincidence when the outbreak occurs.

People who have been told all their lives they're a pain in the ass--guess where they get cancer? People who store up their bad feelings in their stomach--guess where they get cancer? A child who was constantly told he was a "big mouth," "too loud," keep quiet"--guess where he got cancer?

For each percentage *increase* in unemployment in the United States, there are correspondingly more deaths from heart disease and cirrhosis, more suicides, more admissions to state mental health facilities, and the like.

Sociological studies of ghetto life with its overcrowded housing, high levels of unemployment and crime, and noise pollution contribute significantly to stress and poor health.

A life-long friend of mine, Joseph Dahdah, the Postmaster for Feeding Hills, Massachusetts, and his wife were out to celebrate their wedding anniversary. He hadn't seen his best man from his wedding in many years. Seated nearby in the same restaurant is his best man. A coincidence?

One day when I was in the sixth grade I was walking home and took a shortcut through a wooded area I had never passed through before. There I came upon a foundation excavation for a future home site, filled with about four feet of water from the night before. I was astonished to see this little boy-- about five years old--inside the cellar struggling to get out and choking on water. I lay down in the mud and reached inside and pulled him to safety. He sat down on the muddy ground and cried and shook from shock and fear. I attempted to comfort him with an arm around his shoulders an soothing words. When he finally regained his composure, he jumped up and ran home. I never found out who he was. When I got home I caught hell for the mess I was in and nobody wanted to hear any excuses. What do you think? Was it a coincidence I strayed from my usual route?

I'm not sure of the value of attempting to intellectualize the above events. However, I do see benefits in learning to accept "what is" and "what isn't" and in believing there are no coincidences in life. Since internalizing and accepting this belief I've had equisite insights. I see more linking of events and have become increasingly more accurate in predicting the future.

DEATH & DYING/
SEPARATION & LOSS

My third bout with cancer made me face my mortality. Yet it is equally important not to give up, regardless of the prognosis. Continue to be aggressive about getting the best treatment you can get, medical and holisitic.

The doctor said it: CANCER. My mind screamed it: CANCER. Does anyone hear the screams? Anyone at all? Someone, please; someone, listen; hear the unspoken.

With a diagnosis of cancer, the uncertainty of your life, the prospect of your personal time of death, forces upon you a unique philosophical dilemma:

WHAT DO YOU DO IN THE TIME YOU HAVE BETWEEN NOW AND THE TIME YOU DIE?

Time takes on a different meaning for you. Time begins to mean NOW! An organization called Make Today Count started by Orville Kelley is made up of cancer patients who embrace this philosophy, this new way of living, celebrating each day.

The following excerpts are from Dr. Norman Vincent Peale's pamphlet, *An Exciting New Day Every Day:*

You can live an exciting new day every day. That statement may impress you as a rather big order. Well, why not? We do not deal with little orders, but with big orders. We promise you great things in the name of a great God. You can live an exciting new day

every day. This one day, today will be gone
very soon, never to be lived again. It may be
lived in memory, but you and I have this day
only to live today in fact. It is one day out of
a total span of our lives on this wonderful
earth. And the total number of all our days is
not all that great; relatively, they are few in
number. At 80 years of age you will have
lived only 29,220 days. That is all. And if you
live to be 90 you will only have 32,872 days,
counting leap years. That is probably the
maximum you may expect for your life on
earth. Therefore, every day should be taken
in hand, held there like a precious jewel,
viewed as incredibly valuable, thought of as
one marvelous exciting day!

So, every day can be an exciting new day. But
how? This must be a very important question because recently a poll was taken which resulted in a
report that 51 out of every 100 Americans are bored.
Whether this is true or not, I have no way of knowing, for I didn't take the poll myself. My only
comment is that the kind of people I meet do not
talk that way. They wouldn't dare! The report went
on to say that it gets worse with age, for, of the older people polled, "Seventy-five percent of Americans and Canadians over 65 years of age are bored."

Exciting events are taking place, great movements
of a social nature look toward a better world and, for
those who do not have Freedom, ours is thought of
as the greatest country on earth. What do you mean,
bored? What can be the matter with any human
being who is bored when it is possible to have an
exciting day every day?

Well then, how do you keep from being bored?
One answer is--don't think bored. And remember,

you become what you think. If you think bored, you are going to be bored. If you think sick, you are going to be weak. If you think failure, you are going to fail.

So, think excitement! Think God's thoughts after Him. He breathed into you the breath of life and He gave you a mind with which you can think excitedly. And as you think excitedly you create an exciting life for yourself and for those about you.

Just suppose you weren't going to have any more days? Then suppose, when you thought your days were about to run out, you were told that you were going to live--what would you think? There are people who have thought they were to die and then the doctor said to them. "You're going to make it. You're going to live.!" In other words, God said, "I am going to give you some more of those precious days." How would you feel? Wouldn't you be excited?

Of course, the moon has nothing to do with it-- neither have the stars, nor your horoscope, nor the sign under which you were born. The only thing that has anything to do with your life is what you, yourself, with God's help, determine to make of it. You can live an exciting life if you get excited in your thoughts. Greet every day as a new gift from God, a magnificent opportunity.

It doesn't make any difference, either, what the weather is. It's what the weather is in your mind that determines the climate of the day. So, why don't you take a piece of paper and write down the number of days you have lived, and then figure out how long you are going to live and look at the few you have left. But every last one of them is a jewel! Every last one of them is wonderful! Make them so by the excitement of God in your life.

But just thinking isn't enough. You must do some experiencing to make the days of your life exciting.

I learned to give up a lot of old behaviors and feelings:

"Don't do this! Don't do that! It might involve pain. It's too risky, too chancy. You might be rejected. Be satisfied if there's not too much pain, nor too much joy. Keep to the middle of the road and walk with your head bowed to miss the barbs coming your way. What if...if only..."

Death is unknown to the living. There's no one around who can tell you what being dead feels like, although there is mounting information from near-death experiences.

Please let me share a very significant learning for me in my cancer journey, and I'm sure others have reached the same conclusion. I ended up not so worried about dying. The real "bummer" is to die *without* having fully lived. That's the real cheat! My God, I've only been partially alive up to now. I suffered from what too many people suffered: THE FEAR OF LIVING!

An analogy that was used when I did my Erhardt Seminar Training (E.S.T.) was one about people living their lives like someone trying to drive a car and steering with the rear view mirror. They can't, or won't, get into the here and now of life. The past is no longer with us; the future hasn't arrived; therefore, the only time you can really live is now, in the moment.

Painful as it may seem, let go of the past. Stop carrying those pictures around in your heart--of past relationships; of what life was like; or could have been, and stop bringing them into the present and trying to fit the present/now into those past pictures.

It doesn't fit. Of course it doesn't because things are constantly changing without our doing anything about it. We continue to invest incredible amounts of energy to get the "now" to fit our fantasized pictures of the past.

Everyday I listen to the radio, television, or hi-fi system I hear a song that I once sang. I become nostalgic. I begin to think "if only", "what if"--and start to get depressed. I must give that up. I can't live my life that way. Time is too precious. I can't afford to kill it.

A number of years ago I was in a community theatre production of the musical *Milk and Honey*. The two romantic leads are middle-aged people and the man sings the following to the current love of his life:

Let's not waste a moment,
Let's not lose a day,
There's a short forever,
Not too far away.
We don't have to hear the clock remind us,
that there's more than half of life behind us;
When you face a soft forever,
There's no right or wrong,
I can only face forever if you come along.
I can only find my way if you're
there to lead me on.
So let's not waste a moment,
Oh look another moment's gone.

Most of us are stuck, trapped into thinking too much about having a good time or a bad time. We do this with our relationships, wants, wishes for the future. A critical point I'm making is this: get out of thinking so much and start experiencing. Connect up affect with effect and then get out of your mind and encounter the "now". When's the last time you derived pleasure from an ice cream cone? Remember? You really savored it. You weren't thinking, "Let's see now, how am I going to enjoy this? How can I make this a pleasurable experience?" You just enjoyed it. Life is short no matter how long you live...so live!

In spite of my criticisms of the medical profession, I hold physicians in high esteem. I respect and understand them probably more than I verbalize. Consider the fact that doctors are trained to be "mechanics" and "life-savers". However, every generation has one hundred percent death. If you take on the responsibility of being a life-saver and everybody dies, you are bound to be adversely affected.

Intellectually we all know we are going to die someday. Emotionally we choose to deny the fact. I found that by confronting my death openly, it freed more energy for getting well and getting on with the process of living. A number of friends, family members, and acquaintances who mourned my death prematurely are now dead. I find that interesting yet take no pleasure from the fact. What frightened a lot of my associates is the fact that they were forced to think about their own finite existence here on Earth. "Good heavens, if this could happen to Ray, could it happen to me too?"

I'm absolutely convinced that you won't ever "get your act together" until you deal with death on a personal level. Pardon the skepticism, but when I hear some people saying, "I got my act together," that's all they've got. If they haven't shared in the death of someone dear they'll never get it together. If we had unlimited time on earth, if there were no end to physical life, then life would have little meaning. Death reminds us that our time is limited. We better get the job done, accomplish some purpose here on earth, because we don't have forever. Even those people who believe in reincarnation say, "You better do it right now because you're going to come back and face it again and again until you get it right."

Ernest Becker, who wrote a wonderful book entitled *The Denial of Death* said, "Man is a creature whose nature is to try to deny his creatureliness." He also said, "Each of us constructs a personality, a style of life or, as Wilhelm Reich said, a character armor in a vain effort to deny the fundamental fact of our animality. We don't want to admit that we stand alone. So we identify with a more powerful person, a cause, a flag, or the size our bank account."

From my personal experience with cancer, and my observation and engagements with many other cancer patients, those people who have a belief in some kind of afterlife appear to be in a better emotional state, facing the fact of death much more easily.

I have come full-circle in my belief system. I was reared a Roman Catholic, then came close to atheism and settled into agnosticism. Now I'm still raising questions about the ethereal sphere. I believe in some power greater than mankind I call God. I believe there is life after death, and science, rather than disproving this, is proving it. All matter is energy, and you can't destroy energy. All you can do is transform it--change water to steam, change fossil fuels, like coal and oil, to heat. Why not the same for humankind? I refuse to believe we just die, and that's the end of it all. I want to believe we undergo transformation.

I heard my friend Dr. Bernard Siegel quote an old Indian saying, "When you were born, you cried, and the world rejoiced. When you die, the world cries, and you rejoice."

Gerald G. Jampolsky, M.D., the founder of the center for Attitudinal Healing, said, "Each moment offers you a gift. The more you live in the present, the more love, joy and inner peace you experience.

I think that facing death squarely, confronting it in a personal way, allows you to grow and appreciate your uniqueness as no other experience can.

This very moment, I suggest, might be a good time for you, the reader, to stop reading this and get into your own thoughts; make contact with your spirit, internalize some feelings about life, death, and living.

Think about this for a minute: If you were told you were going to die in a matter of days or weeks, what would you do? Part of what I did was take a hard look around me and examine what's really important. My list is extensive. What's most important is that *in the process of doing this I was really alive*. Never more really alive.

Should people be allowed to die at home in the "living room?" Lawrence LeShan, in *The Mechanic and the Gardener,* wrote:

> Medicalization has gone so far that we no longer even believe in our ability to die alone or in the warmth of the company of our loved one. We feel that we must have around us a court of white-coated antiseptic figures to make the final transition. The individual has come to feel so helpless that he cannot even wrestle with his own death or find his own path to it.

Dr. Melvin Krant, professor of medicine at Tufts University Medical School said, "The citadel of medical progress, the hospital, ironically becomes a center of frustration and conflict when confronted with the dying patient. On one hand, most Americans, separated from death most of their lives, call on the hospital for professional skills to help the dying patient. On the other, the mainstream work of the hospital, which places greatest value on cure or rehabilitation, leads away from the dying patient."

I find it disturbing that so many families of the cancer patients I've seen refused to even discuss the possibility of allowing the cancer patient to die at home. The patient isn't even given a "vote". I feel disturbed by this selfishness and lack of awareness. I ask you, "Whose needs should come first?" Too often, it's not the patients.

When I've suggested to family members that they consider bringing their kin home to die, resistances and defences go up, and I hear things like:

"Whatever you do, Ray, please don't suggest that to my mother."

"We can't bring him home; it would be too upsetting to Grandma."

"It would be too hard on us all."

"We don't know how to care for her."

The person who cannot, or will not, contemplate his own death feels most uncomfortable with someone who is dying. This is true of both physicians and lay people.

When I was a kid growing up in the 1930's and 1940's, I attended a number of funerals, all in the homes of the dead. I don't like the fact that we seem less and less prepared to accept the care of dying patients in our homes. "We don't have the time, the space, the knowledge, the manpower," ad nauseam. I wonder! By ignoring the dying, are we attempting to shut ourselves off from the experience of death?

I've experienced both professional and lay people who won't speak the words "cancer" or "died". They'll use euphemisms. One of my doctors skirted using the word "cancer." When June's mother died I was told by one of the nurses that my mother-in-law "expired." I was stunned and said, "You mean she died?" She replied, "That's what I said--she expired."

Several years ago I saw a documentary film on the Public Broadcasting System regarding death and dying. There was one particularly poignant scene where a mother, with her newborn baby, wanted to visit the dying father of the baby. Hospital rules didn't permit visitation rights to children so that mother hid her baby under a poncho-like coat and went to visit her husband. The scene that moved me to tears showed the young mother nursing her baby and holding her husband's hand at the same time. The symbolism of the cycle of life and death was hauntingly beautiful. I am reminded of a couple of lines of poetry (sorry I don't know the author):

"Hope like the tides rises and falls.

Love is like the ocean, constant and forever."

My mother began showing signs that she was ready to part this material/secular world. She was ninety years old--her birthday--and she said to me, "Raymond, my son, I'm tired." This was not the usual spirited, animated, dancing-and-singing Mother I knew all of my life, especially at a celebration. The symbolism and meaning she conveyed hit me gently. She had completed her task. She had raised twelve children with an unlimited supply of love and devotion. She was ready to join my Dad, sister, and two brothers, who preceded her.

When I started to alert my brothers and sisters to the idea that Mom was ready to leave us, there was naturally some resistance to letting her go. We all wanted to keep her here as long as we could, and at the same time we accepted her willingness to go to heaven shortly. Two years later she had a stroke on Thursday and died on Saturday.

A remarkable woman, this fat, short, cherry-nosed Diamond Barbieri Berte. She could not read or write but taught us so much about life and living.

A couple of examples are in order. One day my sister Anita asked Mom how she coped with the daily fears of five sons in World War II, one in the Korean War, and one in the Vietnamese War, plus the experience of three children dying before her, which is not the natural order of things.

Mom's reply was, "Any day you wake up in the morning, see the sky and maybe the sun, and hear the birds singing, it's a beautiful day."

When Ma was dying the family gathered around her en masse. We all continued to touch her and speak to her as if she were fully conscious. My brothers and sisters worked out a time schedule so that one of us would be at her side until the end came. One day my sister Anita and I were talking at Ma's bedside and expressed to Ma that when she joins Pa soon, please give him our love and best wishes. Ma began to tremble and started tapping with one hand her finger tips on the back of Anita's hand. We knew she was trying to communicate something to us relevant to our request regarding Pa. Ma gave the "thumbs down" sign. "What does that mean, Ma? Aren't you going to heaven?" She then gave the "thumbs up" sign. "Then you are expecting to go to heaven." Again she gave the "thumbs up" signal. "And Pa, where will be?" And she gave the "thumbs down" gesture. Even in the process of dying she found a way to share a good chuckle with us.

When she died on Saturday morning, June and Jennifer were with her. "Nifer" phoned me with the news. I went outside and sat on the doorstep, deep in thought and mournfulness. Through my tears I saw the most beautiful hummingbird I have ever seen--almost beak-to-nose. I could have reached out and touched it, and I had the strongest sense that that fragile, divine bird was not afraid of me and was a messenger of peace. You see, birds were among the most favored creatures of the world, according to my Mother. I know this sounds awfully ethereal-- but I take comfort in the thought, and chose to believe, that my Mother made contact through that delicate bird.

Please indulge me one more story regarding my Mother. I think it's the ultimate tribute to a great woman. Any time my family would get together--no matter what the occasion--my brothers and sisters would argue over who was Ma's favorite child. They all sincerely believed that they were the chosen one. Each would communicate something to the effect, "You'd better believe, Buster, it was me." It's O.K. with me if they go on believing that; however, my Mother and I both knew I was her favorite.

I think a few words about the so-called "Conspiracy of Silence" is appropriate at this time.

Sociologists Barney Glaser and Anselm Strauss studied the mutual pretense that often exists when patient and staff know the patient is dying. (I will add patient and family to this conspiracy). Keep the conversations on safe ground. Talk about the disease but skirt its fatal significance. Stick to safe topics-- anything that signifies life going on as usual.

This is a fragile pretense, but not one that either party can easily break. Glaser and Strauss found that patients would sometimes send cues to the staff and family that they wanted to talk about dying, but the nurses, doctors, and family members would decide not to talk openly with them because they feared the patient would break up. The patient would openly make a remark acknowledging his or her death, but these others would ignore it. Then out of tact or empathy for the embarrassment of distress he/she caused, the patient would resume his/her silence. Family and medical staff would breath a sigh of relief, and their uneasiness would maintain the pretense with everyone suffering and losing.

The reverse stance is also true. A doctor or family member may give the patient an opening to talk about dying and have the patient ignore it. I agree with Elisabeth Kubler-Ross's suggestion: let the patient know you are available and willing to talk about dying--or anything else for that matter--but not to force the subject on the patient. When he/she no longer needs to deny death, the patient will seek out a sympathetic ear and open the topic.

There are some dying patients who chose to deny right to the end. Some well-intentioned people will feel the need to cut through this denial. I think this is a no-no. This behavior is forcing your values on someone else. It doesn't serve the patient who chooses to deny. Death with dignity also means being allowed to die in character. If the patient insists on being macho and stoic, then that's O.K. If they want to mourn privately, that's O.K. too. If they want to deny death publicly, that too is the patient's perogative.

Elisabeth Kubler-Ross says, "What the dying teach us is how to live." In summing up what she has learned from her dying patients, she likes to recite a poem by Richard Allen that goes:

"...as you face your death, it is only the love
you have given and received which will count
...if you have loved well then it will have been
worth it
...but if you have not death will always come
too soon and be too terrible to face."

When my wife's Mother died, her Dad became
extremely critical and harsh toward June. Of the
three children in the family, June had been the most
loving and available to her Mother. Why, now, was
her father so upset with her? I think it was an emotional release. He was feeling guilty and inadequate;
looked around to see where he could lay the blame
for his feelings and chose his daughter.

Too many people feel guilty at the death of
someone they know and love. "I should have been
kinder; I could have been more helpful; I didn't
show enough attention", etc. I mention this because
I don't want anyone feeling guilty at my death. I
forgive all the real and imaginary insults and hurts.
Should the death process take an extended time, it's
O.K. for my family and friends to feel relief without
guilt. There's nothing wrong about feeling relieved
of the pain and mental distress and economic pres-
sures.

Some folks will be upset if they notice relief in
family members. To hell with them. Be as honest
as you dare to be. I would love dancing, singing, and
feasting. Those who have loved me will experience
their sadness and sense of loss in their own time and
in their own way.

I had this terrible experience of a child drowning
at the summer camp I directed. I'll never forget
holding this dead boy and seeing one of my junior
counselors laughing. She had a look of stark terror
in her eyes, yet she was laughing. A newspaper

reporter telephoned me and wanted the story she had heard about the "insensitive laughing counselor."

I asked the reporter if she had ever been in a situation where it was difficult for her to control her emotions. Haven't you ever seen happiness appear as tears? How about love and hate getting tangled together? Does it seem so strange that in the presence of death we feel a great confusion of emotions? What would anyone want, or expect, from an innocent, fourteen-year-old, facing this kind of experience?

Resources appeared during my darkest hours of despair...loving, caring individuals ready to share some of the burden and agony I was experiencing. My wife and children, brothers and sisters, friends, students, and clients all communicated their concern. While I was in the hospital I received dozens of get well cards, mass cards, telegrams, and phone calls. One of my students, with tears pouring down his face, entreated me, "Fight, Ray. Fight like hell and get well. Lean on me."

Elisabeth Kubler-Ross says the first significant lesson in her life was that it takes *one human being who really cares* to make a difference between life and death. It would be so wonderful if all of us would give "live" messages without reservations--to help instill more humanity in a world full of inhumanity. Really, dear reader, it takes very little effort to make a big difference in someone's life.

DRIVEN vs. MOTIVATED

Knowing the shortness of life on a gut level makes every day precious. To live abundantly becomes a central goal.

When you are not affirmed or validated as a child, you grow up with feelings of unworthiness. Some of us try to overcome our feelings of unworthiness by overcompensation. We do too much of a good thing. Instead we need to re-educate ourselves, adopting a more tolerant mode that lets us take care of our own needs.

Most cancer patients examine the quality of their lives. One of the first people I heard speak about quality vs. quantity of life was a teenage volunteer working in a cancer treatment program. I was invited by the American Cancer Society to address a young audience of these volunteers at the University of Delaware. During the conference this young woman said, "I'm much more concerned with adding life to years, than years to life." Another example of the wisdom of youth.

I did a lot of thinking, and even more feeling, about that kind of deep, philosophical concept. One very important conclusion I reached was that I wasn't *motivated* to live; I was being *driven* to destruction.

Shortly after my third outbreak of cancer I attended a workshop under the direction of Hedges Caper. Mr. Caper is a psychotherapist in the San Diego, California area and one of the early trainers in the application of transactional analysis. Mr. Caper took the "driver" concept promulgated by Tabbie

Kailer and refined Kailer's work with "allowers."

It's my belief that the vast majority of people who seek counseling or other type of outside help aren't so much interested in or desirous of changing as they are hungry for validation: show me that I'm an O.K. person; that I count; that there's a purpose to my being here in the world; that I'm capable and lovable.

It is extremely rare for any of us to communicate that we are feeling unwanted, unworthy, or unloved. What is more likely to be communicated is, "Your hair is a mess. Can't you prepare a decent breakfast?" The fact that he got shot down the night before when he made amorous overtures to his wife doesn't get discussed. Substitute feelings of frustration and anger get communicated with "attack behavior." What he's really feeling is unloved. At bottom, all negative feelings are interconnected, flowing from feeling unwanted, unworthy, unloved.

At some time, and at some level of consciousness, your kin and closest friends realize you aren't going to make it in this world the way things are going. They've blown it, and they want you to make it. The prescription they come up with, undoubtedly zapped into them, is the five "drivers." Let's face it, though. First they get you "sick"; otherwise, why would you need a prescription?

The diagram below shows one of the ways we get sick to begin with, driven rather than motivated.

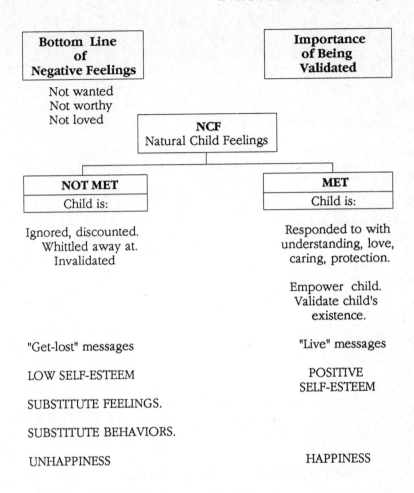

Bottom Line of Negative Feelings	Importance of Being Validated

Not wanted
Not worthy
Not loved

NCF
Natural Child Feelings

NOT MET	MET
Child is:	Child is:

Ignored, discounted.
Whittled away at.
Invalidated

Responded to with
understanding, love,
caring, protection.

Empower child.
Validate child's
existence.

"Get-lost" messages

"Live" messages

LOW SELF-ESTEEM

POSITIVE
SELF-ESTEEM

SUBSTITUTE FEELINGS.

SUBSTITUTE BEHAVIORS.

UNHAPPINESS

HAPPINESS

A number of things happen to open the doors to either unhappiness or happiness. Primarily, we make decisions–life-affecting decisions about ourselves, about others, about life and about how to survive in a chaotic world. Not having been accepted, appreciated and approved as children we have low self-esteem. We over compensate with unreasonable expectations of ourselves, exacting the impossible. We do not allow ourselves to be human. Some decisions give us a diminished life; others an *abundant* life.

DIMISHED LIFE	DECISIONS	ABUNDANT LIFE
5 Drivers 1. Please me. 2. Hurry up. 3. Try harder. 4. Be perfect. 5. Be strong.	Accept as a "given" that we all have the ability to make decisions and we do.	*Allowers* 1. It's O.K. to please your-self sometimes. 2. It's O.K. to take whatever time you need. 3. It.s O.K. to use and develop your abilities. It's O.K. to be sucessful. 4. It's O.K. to make mistakes. Accept your humanness and fallibility. 5. It's O.K. to feel whatever you're feeling.

In and of themselves, the drivers are not bad. As with any virtue that gets carried to an extreme and becomes a fault, so, too, do the drivers. They are a way of coping and surviving in this world. The problem is they can exact too high a price.

Let's discuss the unwholesome side of the drivers.

Driver 1 - PLEASE ME

We learn early in life that one way to survive is to

figure out how to please our parents. That's not bad–except when carried to extremes and generalized to too many other people and situations. We begin by pleasing Mom and Dad. Then we please our friends, our teachers, our employers, our in-laws, and so on. We can become over-adapted, impotent "nice guys/gals" who become "floaters" in life. "Floaters" are very comfortable to have around. Why shouldn't they be...they don't have opinions of their own. They wait for you to express yours and then agree with it. They very rarely say "no" to anyone.

"Let me borrow your car."

Sure.

"Loan me a ten spot."

O.K.

"Hey, buddy, come on over for a drink. I need some company."

Gee, I don't know. It's 2:30 in the morning.

"You saying no to me?"

No, No, I'm not saying no to you. I'll be right over.

And so it goes.

A favorite anecdote of mine that typifies the "please me" driver is as follows: A little Arab was leading his donkey through the market place. As he passed a group of people they made negative remarks about his stupidity in overloading his burro. Not wanting to displease them he took the load off the donkey and carried it on his own shoulders and proceeded on his way. Another group of villagers ridiculed him, "How dumb can you be? Don't you know burros were made to carry things and you, dummy, you carry them." Listening to this new input, the Arab shifts the load back to the donkey. This happened several times until the harrassed little

Arab decided to avoid everyone and took a path up
the mountain around the market place, a path he had
never travelled before. The road narrowed and
twisted up the mountain and finally became so
cramped the donkey fell to its death at the bottom
of the ravine. What's the moral of this story? If you
try to please everyone, you'll lose your ass.

There is fine print in the contract of life that says,
"You can't please everyone," but most of us don't
bother to read it.

An educator was once asked, "What's the secret
of success?" He replied he didn't know, but he did
know the secret of failure: "Try to please everyone." It can't be done.

Driver 2 - TRY HARDER
Sound familiar? I'll bet it does. We've all been
"zapped" with this one. Try harder. You're not
trying hard enough."

Now what's wrong with this? Shouldn't we try?
Of course we should. Not to try could be the
biggest mistake of our lives. What I'm referring to
here is a concept of trying that does nothing but
create paralysis of action or poor performance.

The word "try" has a very seductive quality about
it. We learned the lesson very well as children: if
we wanted to get someone off our backs, just say,
"I'll try." When your parents suggested you do this,
do that, join that club or group, you would reply,
"I'll try, Mom and Dad." They would accept your
"I'll try" for "I will."

We think it's motivational to drive people with
"try harder," try harder." Usually, all "trying harder"
does is create tension and ineffective performance
because we're trying too hard. Did you ever try to
hit a golf ball, tennis ball, or a baseball? The harder

you tried the worse your performance. You became too tense and your learned, or natural, ability suffered.

When was the last time you tried to relax? It didn't work. So you tried harder? Maybe if you didn't try so hard, it would just happen. What happens to the man caught in quicksand who struggles to get out? The harder he tries, the more he sinks into the mire.

The best teachers and coaches I've ever met teach a simple and most effective way. They take a complicated skill and break it down into smaller components. Then they work with you as you perfect each part until it becomes tacit knowledge (i.e., becomes like second nature) and you don't think about how to hit the fast ball; you just do it. The teacher/coach doesn't say, "Try to hit it; try to play the game right." They help remove the obstacles to your ability to perform. They teach you to relax and give up doing it wrong. They communicate it's O.K. to succeed; it's O.K. to use your talents and develop your capacities. Put some effort into it without the "try harder" driver.

There have been numerous occasions when a client would make an agreement with me that he/she would practice a new behavior during the week between our counseling sessions. I would remind my client, as he/she was leaving about our contract. The client would say something like, "You bet." I'll try, Ray." Stop! I motion him back into the room and ask him to repeat what he just said. The client will defend and protect; all I said was, "I'll try."

I then use an approach that many Transactional Analysis therapists use (I also saw it similarly used in my Erhart Seminar Training (E.S.T.). Using some common object in the room, such as a paperweight or key ring, I ask my client to "pick up the weight." After picking it up, I ask him to put it back on the desk. Once again I ask "pick it up" and he'll do it again. Then I ask, "*try* to pick it up." Usually he will pick it up again. I ask again, "*try* to pick it up." Sooner or later he won't pick it up and I point this out to him saying, "Sometimes you pick it up and when you don't want to do that you won't pick it up. Do you have the ability to pick up the weight? Of course you do. You don't try to pick it up. You either will or you won't. You either have the ability or you don't. Now then, let's talk some more about your homework. Can you do it? Will you do it? Don't give me any crap about 'I'll try'."

I suggest we do away with "try" in our vocabularies.

Driver 3 - HURRY UP

Hurry up. Hurry up. Hurry up, kid, you're not moving fast enough. Come on; I have to go. I don't have time to stop. Have to run along. Go, man go. I'm late. I wanted it yesterday. Hurry up.

We do crazy things with this driver. We don't enjoy where we are, because we're in a hurry to go somewhere else. We don't appreciate and be *with* whomever we're with because we're in a hurry to be with someone else. We don't take the time to taste our food, or smell the flowers along the way.

What happens when you get behind the wheel of your car and tromp on the gas pedal? The tires spin until you let up on the gas; then you generate momentum and move on. The same principle applies with all drivers. When you ease off, you become more efficient, able to accomplish more and perform better. With the increased efficiency you meet deadlines without the "hurry up."

I've found in some marriages with sexual dissatisfaction that a contributing factor often is that one partner has a "hurry up" driver. "O.K., O.K., get it over with. I've got other things to do."

Insomniacs suffer from a "hurry up" driver. They jump into bed, pull up the bed covers, and drive themselves: "Got to get to sleep. Hurry up. Got to get to sleep."

In 1965 I went to California to meet Dr. Eric Berne and other well-known transactional analysts and get some training in this therapeutic method. Some of my friends and I went to Sequoia National Park and I was overwhelmed with the natural wonders of the place...the giant trees, the beautiful flowers, the magnificent wild life...there really is a God. At one point I was standing in a cool mountain stream looking around at all the wondrous sights and suddenly I became aware of station wagons, recreational vehicles and the like, driving hell bent for leather *through* the Park. I wondered aloud to my friends, "Wonder where they're rushing to?" Their vehicles were covered with stickers proclaiming all the places they had visited. You may catch up with some of them at the "tourist trap" buying more stickers. They were rushing through Sequoia to get to Yosemite, and when they arrive at Yosemite they'll be in a hurry to get to Yellowstone. Can't you hear them when they arrive back home? "Oh yes, we went to this place, we saw that, etc." They never took the time to *experience* any of it. They were in too much of a hurry.

The "hurry up" driver is ubiquitous: Beauty contests for elementary school-age kids; little boys and girls dressed like adults; caps and gowns for nursery school graduation; boy-girl parties for fifth graders; keg parties for junior high school kids; all night dances and parties for tenth graders. I know of pregnant women who shop around for the best nursery schools to get their yet unborn children on the fast track. Hurry up, kid.

A particularly repugnant memory of mine is the time June and I were attending a New Year's Eve party and the neighbor of the host showed up with her five-year-old daughter dressed in a negligee and peignoir. This woman proceeded to show off her creation and boast with pride about "how sexy my little beauty is." I felt like throwing up.

Driver 4 - BE PERFECT

Maybe you're having a sympathetic reaction to this one. Oh my, we do have to be perfect, don't we? Anything less than perfect and we feel destroyed.

This is one of the easiest drivers of all to be programmed, and it starts very early. What happened when you came home from school with a report card that had 4 A's and 2 B's? What did everyone focus on? Yes, I know. I remember all those times when I'd come home from playing Little League Baseball and Pa or one of my older brothers would ask me how I did that day. If I said I went two for four he would say, "Is that all?" If I had a four for four day (four hits in four times at bat) he would ask, "What were they?" Two doubles and two singles. He would respond "What, no home runs?"

This is another example of that small print in the contract of life: "It'll never be enough!" Can't you see it? A child picks some wild flowers to give a bouquet to Mom and Dad. As she stands in front of them proudly presenting them with her loving gift, they respond, "It's lovely, darling, but you're standing on the grass."

You could characterize the life of "losers" with,"Is that all?" There's a fraternal organization in this country where the prerequisite for membership is you must have accumulated a million dollars before your fortieth birthday. Most of the members are "losers" at life. Inside their heads they hear voices saying, "Is that all?" They could have earned ten million, ten billion, and still hear the voices saying, "Is that all?" It will never be enough. You'll always be standing on the grass.

When June and I went to pick up Keith, our first adopted child, we arrived at the Diocesan Bureau and were presented with this tiny baby who had a three-inch-wide strip of gauze diagonally wrapped around his skull covering one ear. When we questioned the reason for the bandages, we were told Keith was born with one ear that protruded from his head and some of the adoption authorities were concerned we wouldn't take him. To what extreme do we carry this absurd drive to "be perfect?" As June and I looked at this extremely beautiful baby, filling us with love, June very gently removed the gauze and snuggled him to her breast, and said, "We'll take him, bent ear and all!"

Please don't misunderstand me. I think it's desirable to strive for perfection. The difficulty arises when we are driven to the *neurotic pursuit of the perfection* that denies our humanness, our fallibility. We all make mistakes and should be *allowed* to do so. We learn from our mistakes; we profit from them; we risk and grow from them. If we feel we must be perfect, the fear and humiliation of making mistakes stops us from risking any potential growth. "Better I keep my mouth shut and keep up my facade, my cool image, rather than risk failure.

I think former President Richard Nixon may have

a "be perfect" driver stuck in overdrive. He made human mistakes. He listened and followed some poor advisors. Rather than admit to his errors, President Nixon felt the need to cover up and succeeded in compounding his mistakes. I think if he had appealed to the reasonableness and compassion in the American public very early in the Watergate mess, the majority would have forgiven him. However, he had to be perfect. Think back to all the comedians and imitators of Mr. Nixon and you'll recall a recurring line of dialogue that wasn't a coincidence: "Let me make this perfectly clear." Like the rest of us, the poor man felt he had to be perfect.

I hope this doesn't confuse you too much, but I believe we were all born "perfect"--in spite of our shortcomings, our deficiencies, our bent ears. *We are perfect if we become what we were meant to become.* However, we are *led* to believe that we are something other than that perfection. We are led to believe we are stupid, unfeeling, uncaring, uncreative. These evaluations are not true. You were led to believe that about yourself. Harry Stack Sullivan referred to it as "reflected appraisal." R. D. Laing spoke about the "process of attribution." The "trips" start to get laid on you early: you internalize them and you become them. Too bad. You were meant to be perfect. Perfectly yourself. Abraham Maslow suggested "self-actualization" as one of the best goals in life. Find that perfection you were meant to be. Learn to self-validate. The ideal self has always been there inside you. It is ignorance, fear--and often greed--that destroys our real self.

Driver 5 - BE STRONG

The "be strong" driver has corollaries like, "be a man," "be a woman," "big boys don't cry," "you shouldn't feel that way," etc. Got the picture?

This is a particularly destructive driver because it makes us want to deny our feelings, or at least to negotiate them (i.e., if I shouldn't feel what I'm feeling, what is permitted me?)

We have been conditioned to avoid negative feelings. We learned early in life that if we cried, or got angry, we could avoid issues. Most of us never learn to use anger to solve problems. Some feelings are permitted and others must be denied. If you dared express jealousy, envy, bashfulness, rancor and the like, there was always someone quick to tell you, "You mustn't feel that way!" Talk about a denial of reality. Sometimes I do feel that way.

I could recount story after story to illustrate this driver. Two cases in point, one rather humorous story that sheds light on how mundane and insidious this driver can be, and another example, more dramatic and obvious. The less graphic instance was the time my family went to a picnic and I heard June say to our daughter, "I'm getting cold. Jennifer, put on a sweater." Because she's feeling cold, she assumes our daughter must also be cold. "Feel what I feel." A more histrionic example was the time I was sitting in the living room of a psychiatrist friend. His seven-year-old son John was riding his bike when Billie, the kid next door, kicked John's front wheel and John had a nasty fall. He ran into the living room, where we were sitting, and his Dad began to minister to his wounds. John was crying and saying things like, "It hurts, Dad. Dad, look I'm bleeding right through my trousers. Dad, my shirt is ripped." Mr. "Psychiatrist" seemed impervious to his son's pleading until John said, "You know what, Dad, I feel like going next door and killing that Billie." Dad responded with, "Oh, John, you're not mad. You're just tired." Here we go again: Don't feel what you're feeling. Feel what I tell you to feel. Deny your true feelings.

Rarley do I use the word "never," but I do urge you to *never* deny anyone's feelings. *Never* ask anyone to negotiate their feelings. If you want to help them, relate to the issues, thoughts and ideas behind the feelings; what's going on under those feelings. Validate them.

In order to move from unhappiness to happiness, from diminished to abundant life, you need first to make a decision to move. "I don't like it here and I want to go there." This requires practicing new behaviors. I am not suggesting radical changes. For example, if you have a "please me" driver, set aside one evening, one morning, or perhaps one day a week just to please yourself. Experience yourself saying "no"; "I don't want to"; and don't apologize. It's O.K. to be assertive and have your wants and needs come first, at least part of the time. So, with the new decision to move and to practice new behaviors you'll generate momentum toward happiness. You'll start your trip to an abundant life. I wish you "good journey."

A NEW LIFESTYLE

PART 3

HOLISM

Modern medicine has accomplished tremendous successes in treating many diseases and the advances in surgery have been nothing short of miraculous. On the other hand, modern medicine has typically failed to treat the whole person. I'm absolutely convinced that the holistic model, which addresses the needs of the whole body, the mind, and the spirit is the way to promote health.

Holism? What is this thing called holism? Is it some kind of cult with a guru? Is it a religion? Should doctors be afraid of it? Is it sitting inside a triangular configuration with a magnetic field? Or studying the heavenly bodies?

I know a well-known physician in the western Massachusetts area, a highly respected surgeon, who felt the need to stand up at a large meeting of local citizens deeply involved in community health concerns and warned them about some new doctors in the area who were practicing holistic medicine. "Can you imagine...licensed doctors advocating holism? Some of those in attendance were led to believe that these "new kids on the block" were using witchcraft, were lacking in integrity, and were probably charlatans, at best.

Communication between this doctor and me would be most difficult, probably impossible. We're coming from different value systems. He sees himself as a healer. I say we have to heal ourselves. He wants his patients passive to his authority, unquestioning about his knowledge. He has an excessive need to be in control of doctor-patient relationship. I won't allow my "vote" to be cancelled, especially if I'm going to be affected by the decision.

When we get sick, we feel bad all over. We feel the loss of energy, slowed down, "stressed out," and out-of-balance. When one part of you suffers, your whole body feels it.

Holistic health is really a very old concept, reminding us of the unity of life and the essential oneness of all systems. True healing is an affirmation of our wholeness. We are spirit, mind, and body. All are equally important.

Everything affects our health: physical, emotional, spiritual, environmental. All are interconnected in some way and affect one another.

Dr. Bernard Siegel says, "Anytime you get sick, it's your body's way of telling you to take another path." Anytime your life seems to fall out of synchronization, you can bet this disharmony will manifest itself in some bodily complaint.

One of the basic principles of the holistic philosophy is that we create our own realities. As we perceive and experience, we interpret those experiences and create our subjective realities. Since there is no single remedy, no system, no single healer to treat all our ills, we must take responsibility for our own health, our entire reality. We own our own feelings, thoughts, and behaviors. Don't be afraid, or resist, that concept. It's meant to empower you. It places you at cause in your life rather than at effect. Powerful...accept and believe that you are in control of your body. Listen to it and act upon the messages it sends you regarding the necessity to make changes in your life.

Holistic health is concerned with more than the absence of illness and disease. Holistic medicine focuses on vibrant, joyful wellness that comes from within the person who makes a conscious effort to get it all together, physically, emotionally, mentally, spiritually, and environmentally. Ask most anyone how they feel and they'll answer, "Not bad," "So-so," "O.K." Ask a holistic practitioner and you're more likely to hear, "Fantastic; great; top of the heap."

The concept of holism has been around for thousands of years. Plants, animals, and human beings are more than the sum of their parts. The Greek word "halos" means whole and transposes to the English term "holistic." To understand people you must see them as much more than a collection of muscles, organs, and skin. We tend to overlook the spirit, the spiritual aspects of humankind that gives us balance and harmony.

One of my favorite stories in Greek mythology is the one about gods getting together and trying to decide where they should hide the divinity of mankind.

The challenge to the gods was great: Where can we hide it so man will never be able to find it? One of the gods suggested placing this godliness of man inside a volcano but that was quickly rejected by the others as "too easy for mankind to find." More proposals followed, such as placing man's perfection/supreme virtue under the sea, buried under mountain ranges, and the like.

All were cast aside with the same complaint: "Too easy; too easily located by man." Finally, one of the gods asked for this genius, this beautiful spirit of man and it was placed in his hands. This god suddenly clapped his hands together with man's deity between them and in a puff of smoke man's divinity disappeared. The other gods were amazed and mystified and asked, "Where did it go? What did you do with it?" The answer was simply, "I placed this excellence of mankind inside man himself. He'll never think to look for it there."

Hindus use the word NAMASTE in greeting family, friends, and acquaintances. My understanding of this term is that it translates into English meaning, "The god/the light in me salutes the god/the light in you."

If you were asked, "What's the largest industry in the world today?" How would you answer the question? Most people would give one of the following: the automobile industry; General Motors; the oil industry; U. S. Steel. Finally someone would tell you, "The military complex; our military defense system." Wrong. Military might cost about a million dollars a day. The medical industry spends about one billion per day and going up. Where will it end? Who will be able to pay their medical costs? As far as I'm concerned, there's only one answer: *Prevention*. Get on board the holistic philosophy express and practice preventive medicine.

Many medicines don't work. The latest studies indicate that one in three babies born in 1985 can expect to develop some form of cancer in their lifetime unless there are breakthroughs in prevention, diagnosis, and cure. Over half the population in the United States has one or more chronic disabling conditions.

I repeat there's only one solution to all of this: *Prevention*: Stop electing to kill yourself. I think it was Dr. Carl Menninger who used the term, "Suicide by the inch" to describe the self-destructive behaviors such as smoking, overeating, and drinking too much.

Only six percent of our population is without medical complaint, highly energized, and in robust health. Are you in this group? You certainly have the capacity to improve. Holistic medicine is the royal road to get on. Happy trails.

DIET

There is much truth in the platitude you are what you eat.

How did I get cancer? Especially, cancer of the throat? I never smoked and rarely drank alcoholic beverages, which are highly suspect in the cause of throat cancer. In the study of vocal technique, I learned how to care for my throat and not abuse the vocal chords. I used the resonances in my head: mastered the ability to sing over a cold and deepen down when necessary. I could coat a musical note with breath to make the tone velvety, sweet, and romantic or pull from the diaphragm and drive the sound off my hard or soft palate to reverberate brassy.

"Think, Ray, think! What contributed to your cancer?" I'm not positive in my conclusions; however, in my opinion, two strong suspicions come to mind: (1) my eating habits, and (2) the poor ways I dealt with stress. I'm sure there were other possible contributing factors, but for the sake of brevity, I'll concentrate only on the above. In this chapter, I'll focus on diet. Stress will be dealt with in a separate chapter.

The subject of nutrition is one of the most controversial subjects I know. Like the subjects of politics and religion, it arouses great emotional responses. As a scientific issue, the medical community becomes almost deranged by the subject: claims and counter-claims, studies that support beliefs and other studies that refute them.

"Experts" all over the place on both sides of the fence. Whom do you believe? My suggestion to the reader is this: Keep an open mind, read, and then take an aggressive posture in finding out and judging for yourself. Get the best medical assistance you can find--even though it's rare in the area of nutrition. I will share with you some of my findings and beliefs. They worked for me. Each individual has to seek out what works for him/her.

I'm not a student of orthomolecular medicine, although I have done some reading on the subject, and I know very little about biochemistry. One thing I do understand is biochemical individuality. We are all different metabolically. Individuality must be considered in diet, diet supplements, and adjustments for optimum health. Cancer prevention and treatment must consider diet and individual metabolism.

One of the most often asked questions of me is, "Aren't you afraid of overdosing on all those vitamins, minerals, and trace-elements you take?" The simple answer for me is "no." I subscribe to a belief that until you've had too much of anything that's good for you, you probably haven't had enough. To put it another way, until you have evidence to the contrary, your body can take more and use it. (I can hear the screams already. "This guy is wacky.") I envision my body as a beaker, and I fill it with all the essentials it needs. One hundred percent of everything. Anything less and you are that much less efficient. Until the first drop spills over the full container, your body is obviously using everything; therefore, my belief that until you show symptoms of overdose, you are in safe territory. Even when overdose symptoms occur, it's easy to cut back.

The human body is made up of about sixty trillion cells. Aside from the central nervous system, these cells are constantly dying off and regenerating.

Approximately every three months you have a "new" body. The current rebuilding of your body comes from the food and liquid you ingest. This reminds me of the computer term "GIGO," which stands for "garbage in, garbage out." If you absorb low quality food, your body will suffer. On the other hand, if you swallow wholesome, good, clean food, you'll produce a toxic-free, energetic body able to resist disease and respond more efficiently to emergencies.

My precancer eating habits were dreadful. Breakfast, if you could call it that, consisted of coffee with three spoons of sugar and a doughnut. Lunch usually was comprised of a hot dog or hamburger and a coke. Dinner occasionally was a nutritious meal. I was giving myself a "double whammy" by one, not getting what my body required and two, by taking in "tons" of refuse that counter balanced what little good I did eat.

The human body possesses this wonderful mechanism of protecting itself that can become pathological when thrown out of balance. When certain organs are not receiving all the essential nutrients they require, they begin stealing from other organs, and the body breaks down. The deadly combination of toxicity and nutrient deficiency opens up the body to the onset of disease, especially metabolic degenerative disease, and I think cancer may be a metabolic disease.

Before I go any further with this subject, I feel the need to say that I can't possibly cover it in one chapter. If I succeed in piquing your curiosity about the matter, I will have achieved my purpose regarding this topic.

Few subjects are more controversial than nutrition. Whom do you believe? The doctors? The

traditional nutritionists? The health food store own-
ers? The food faddists? Whom?

I have acquired lots of information and formulated
many opinions. I've read and researched extensively
and have reaped some partialities. I repeat: I DO
NOT CONSIDER MYSELF AN EXPERT IN NUTRI-
TION. I want to be up front about that so readers of
this book may judge my recital for themselves. I
would urge you to remain skeptical and judgmental.
Most important of all, I repeat: become aggressive
in your own search for knowledge regarding your
health. What are your unique nutritional needs? I
use the word "unique" in its literal sense. There are
basic common denominators in all of us; however,
the amounts of various vitamins, minerals, and trace
elements needed by each of us is different. Our
size and weight, work environment, exposure to
toxins and allergens, what you eat and, even where
the food is grown, your state of health and methods
of dealing with stress, all contribute to your
nutritional needs.

It isn't enough to just get a measure of a particular
nutrient, and if it's low, just take more. The level at
any one moment will, or may, change, and your
needs may double the next hour. You can become
deficient very quickly, especially if all you ingest is
the Recommended Dietary Allowance (RDA). Learn
to provide for your current needs and anticipate
probable requirements. If you take aspirin, it actually forces vitamin C out of your body. Antibiotics
can cause deficiencies in B complex vitamins. Birth
control pills may increase a woman's need not only
for riboflavin but also vitamins A, B, B_6, B_{12}, C, and
E, plus the B vitamin folate and the mineral zinc.

At this time I admit to my partiality for megadoses of vitamins and minerals and certain trace elements, especially for cancer patients. I believe that modern conditions of living make diet supplements on absolute necessity.

There are stock answers from traditional medical practitioners when asked about food supplements. Their responses predictably include some of the following:

1) Eat a varied diet. That's all you need.

2) Get the basic four food groups (meat, grain, fruit and vegetables, dairy products). (A fast-food cheeseburger with ketchup and a slice of pickle; side order of fries and sugary milkshake fulfills the four basic food groups).

3) Don't waste your money on unneeded vitamins.

4) If you use supplements, all you'll end up with is expensive urine.

5) There's real danger in overdosing on those things.

6) Get your minimum daily requirements, and you'll be secure.

No one I know is surprised any more if their doctor gives a negative response to inquiries about nutrition. He/she probably had no more than a three-hour lecture on nutritional deficiencies in medical school. At the risk of boring you, the reader, I repeat: It's up to you to learn what your unique nutritional requirements are and if you need diet supplements.

In some instances, because vitamins do work, I think some medical practitioners are reluctant to promote them. Vitamins give patients power to treat themselves. This may represent a threat to some doctors, who resent giving up any control. And, as I've repeated several times, one thing cancer patients need desperately is some sense of control over their bodies.

In my opinion, to continue to think in terms of RDA (recommended dietary allowance) or MDR (minimum daily requirements) is courting disaster. These are too many contingencies, faced by all of us, nearly everyday, that affect our bodies' nutritional requirements. Some insults are self-imposed, and others are thrust upon us by the environment. Examples of this are: About 25 mg of vitamin C are destroyed by each cigarette smoked; several nutrients are destroyed or rendered null and void by environmental pollutants, such as automobile emissions. Besides, an analogy my friend Alex Rossmann uses is, "Do you want to settle for minimum love? Not me. I want all I can get." The same applies to nutritional requirements: don't settle for MDR or RDA; get the maximum for vibrant good health.

"The RDA's were originally designed to ensure that large segments of the population would not develop serious nutritional deficiencies," notes Alan R. Gaby, M.D., a physician from Kent, Washington. They are, "minimum requirements for minimum health," and in no way do they attempt to answer the question of whether larger amounts can bestow larger benefits, Dr. Gaby says.

One very strong suggestion/rule for peak health: LIVING FOOD FOR LIVING PEOPLE. To put it another way, chemical, artificial, dead foods for plastic people in minimal health. Eat fresh, wholesome food--mostly vegetables in volume with some fish and fowl. Be warned, however, should you opt to eat this way you'll be perceived as a deviant by some people because you will be eating the way most of our grandparents ate. Eat mostly raw, or as near raw as possible, foods. Fish and fowl are best when baked or broiled--not fried. Enzymes are disease fighters, and enzymes predominate in raw foods. The processing of our foods destroys not only the enzymes but also the vitamins and minerals and trace elements we so vitally need.

Your life depends on enzymes. Enzymes come from proteins, and proteins consist of amino acids. There are over eight thousand different enzymes in the human body, each with a specific function. Some are used to aid in digestion, absorption, and assimilation of food. Others help create new cells, new material in our bodies. Some are disease fighters. Nutritional deficiencies inhibit enzyme activity, and the efficiency of your body is thrown out of balance, jeopardizing your health and life.

At this time I think it's important to point out to the reader that the word "essential" can sometimes be misleading. When nutritional experts and writers talk about the importance of essential vitamins and minerals, etc.,they mean these are the substances that cannot be manufactured in your body but must be digested directly from the foods you eat. There are over twenty naturally occurring amino acids. In adult human beings eight are considered essential.

Because a food has protein doesn't mean that source of protein has all the essential amino acids. A "Mickey Donald" hamburger is not sufficient to meet your body's requirements. It's true that Americans eat a lot of protein; however, they're still deficient in lots of amino acids.

When your body needs to rejuvenate tissue (this process is called "anabolic"), the appropriate enzymes must be present, along with vitamins and minerals which are needed to activate the enzymes to do their job. Remember there are over eight thousand enzymes in your body and over eighty percent get activated by certain essential elements that you get only through a diet rich in vitamins and minerals.

If you are deficient in trace minerals in your diet, the special functions performed by the teamwork of trace elements and enzymes will not be adequate to protect you against disease. If the enzymes are dysfunctional because they lack vitamins and minerals, your immune system cannot protect you against bacterial and viral agents.

Most adults require about seventy grams of top-grade protein every day with quality vitamins and minerals. In my precancer days I averaged about twenty grams of protein a day.

Jonathan Wright, M.D. says, "Doctors today are trained to look for singular cures for singular problems. And nutritional therapy just doesn't always work that way. It may correct a specific condition, but it does so by benefiting the entire organism."

"Most physicians see vitamins as being of value only in cases of gross deficiencies. But there are many specific instances of defective enzymes or metabolic abnormalities where more would *be beneficial* (my italics). It's our belief that vitamins and minerals are enzyme inducers and hormone modulators, which means they can promote beneficial metabolic processes with varying amounts given."

When Porter Shimer asked Dr. Wright how he became interested in the subject of nutritional therapy, he answered, "By studying on my own, *after* medical school." And when asked why he used nutritional therapy, in his practice, he replied, "Because it works."

Following my throat surgery, my food had no

taste. My sense of smell was greatly diminished when I became a neck breather. One of the articles I came across regarding nutrition was about zinc. I loaded up on zinc--about one hundred mg daily--and, miraculously, my sense of taste returned in about three days. My taste buds were stimulated and healthy, the aroma of food returned, and eating was again one of life's great pleasures.

Some scientists in Canada made a study of zinc and linked zinc to prostate health. When the prostate becomes enlarged, and if cancer is present, zinc levels are too low.

Dr. Hans Neiper, a Famous German specialist in cancer research and treatment, found a link between zinc deficiency and cancer of the esophagus. He used zinc therapy to control malignant tumor growths with very impressive results. He treated over three thousand cancer patients with zinc as part of the therapy.

At the prestigious Memorial Sloan-Kettering Cancer Center in New York researchers discovered a correlation between low zinc levels, below T-lymphocyte activity, and poor response in chemotherapy. Zinc supplementation was used with favorable results. T-cells were strengthened and multiplied quicker.

As I mentioned before, certain trace minerals are essential and must be present if enzymes are to perform their immunological functions. People need to be tested for zinc deficiency if they have liver problems, poor eating habits, cancer, or absorption problems. Zinc deficiency cannot only make you sick, but also, if you are ill you'll become more ill.

Because we lose so many nutrients through cooking and processed foods, I suggest mineral supplements, including zinc, to those that want to listen.

One last word on zinc. In my opinion, pregnant mothers need added zinc. Some animal research proves that memory and learning impairments occur in the offspring of rats fed diets deficient in zinc. That's enough implication for me to apply the animal study results to humans. The test of the rats showed the impairment in learning continued into adulthood.

Following testimony given at a Senate subcommittee meeting on the subject of nutrition being taught in medical schools, Senator Patrick J. Leahy of Vermont is reported to have remarked, "There was far, far more time in the average medical school spent on the question of malpractice insurance...than there was on nutrition."

Can you imagine! Wow! Current estimates are that six out of ten leading causes of death in the United States are diet-related.

Fat-Soluble vs. Water-Soluble

Vitamins are either fat-soluble or water-soluble. The term "soluble" means "suspended in." There is some danger if you ingest too much fat-soluble vitamins, which are stored in the body's fatty tissues and liver. Overload the liver with fat-soluble sources of vitamins, and the liver will lose its function of detoxifying the body, a potentially lethal situation. The odds against this happening are infinitesimal. However, to be on the safe side, water-soluble vitamins are preferred.

As of the moment, there are thirteen essential vitamins in all: A, thiamine (B), riboflavin (B-2), B-6, B-12, biotin, C, D, E, folacin, K, niacin,and pantothenic acid.

Natural vs. Synthetic (or chemical)

The argument about natural versus synthetic vitamins has been going on for along time with highly respected people on both sides of the issue. It's true your body can't tell the difference between the molecular structure of natural or synthetic vitamins. A vitamin has a particular molecular structure that is the same whether the vitamin is synthesized in a laboratory or extracted from an animal or plant source. There are two very important distinctions, however, that are often overlooked. One, the synthetic vitamins contain too much sugar and starch, and two, natural sources of extract bring with them contributory substances that make the natural sources more valuable for the body's needs. When natural sources of vitamin are used,there is a synergistic effect. This helps the body assimilate more efficiently and assists in other ways. For example, by far the most serious complication from massive amounts of vitamin C is hemorrhage. This is not a rare occurrence among patients with advanced cancer (i.e., terminally ill patients). The explanation reported to me is that if cancer happens to be wrapped around a blood vessel and the cancer shrinks, it may pull on the blood vessel and cause it to rupture. To me this is pretty good proof that vitamin C is effective against cancer, and the risk of hemorrhage is acceptable. However, the addition of bioflavanoids (bioflavanoids, a group of vitamin-like compounds found in nature and associated with vitamin C, increase the vitamin's effectiveness) from natural sources of vitamin C results in stopping these hemorrhages. I'll take the natural sources any day over the synthetic.

As a general rule, get natural vitamins in natural sources. There are still undiscovered vitamins in natural foods. Synthetically processed vitamins, in all probability, are lacking some still unknown trace elements.

Any vitamin made from a natural source may contain, and usually does, more than the vitamin named, just as a vitamin obtained in a whole food contains more than s single nutrient.

Dr. Albert Szent-Gyorgyi, one of the most highly honored and respected scientists in the world and the discoverer of ascorbic acid, did something which fascinated me. He had a patient with strong subcutaneous capillary bleedings. Dr. Szent-Gyorgyi gave an "impure" ascorbic preparation to the patient, and the bleedings were promptly cured. Later on, when Dr. Szent-Gyorgyi had isolated ascorbic acid into a pure form, another patient showed up with a similar bleeding condition. The second patient was given pure ascorbic acid, and it proved ineffective. Conclusion reached: Impure preparation contained other important substances responsible for the therapeutic action which Dr. Szent-Gyorgyi had purified out of it. Using "intuitive guesswork" (I love this phrase and students of mine are aware of it. I encourage people to trust their intuitions. They usually are accurate.), the active substance Dr. Szent-Gyorgyi uncovered was flavanoid. He observed that pure flavanoid promptly cured the bleedings and did so in case after case.

Now years later since Dr. Szent-Gyorgyi's distinguished work, we know that these flavonoids are substances that can help prevent and cure cataract.

While I'm on the subject of Dr. Szent-Gyorgyi, I would like to quote something from his article in *Executive Health:*

> ...the whole idea of vitamins is a paradox and difficult to digest. Everybody knows that

things we eat can make us sick, but it seems utterly senseless to say that something which we have not eaten could make us sick. And this is exactly what a vitamin is: A SUBSTANCE WHICH MAKES US SICK BY NOT EATING IT.

Dr. J. H. Tilden, who lived from 1851 to 1940, practiced medicine for sixty-eight years. He was severely censured by the rest of the medical profession because after the first eighteen years of his practice,he used no medicine. Dr. Tilden believed that accumulating disease-producing toxins was the primary cause of sickness.

To keep good health he taught that toxemia--produced by the buildup of poisonous waste products of the body--must be prevented, and toxemia must be treated to return sick persons to vibrant health.

This makes a lot of sense to me. Most of us stuff ourselves with too much food, over-refined foods loaded with chemicals. Roughly sixty percent of the great American diet is made up of two substances we don't even need: refined sugar and refined flour. We pour so much junk into our bodies the elimination system does not have enough time to detoxify it; therefore, we recycle the waste inside our bodies and become toxic. Elimination falls far short of the body's requirements, and toxins build up in the blood.

Henry G. Bieler, M.D., in his book Food Is Your Best Medicine, concurs with Dr. Tilden. Dr. Bieler states that as a practicing physician for over fifty years he reached three basic conclusions as to the cause and cure of disease:

(1) Disease is caused by toxemia, which results in cellular impairment and breakdown. In that way, germs multiply because the condition of the toxic

body makes it easier for this to happen.

(2) In almost all cases, the use of drugs in treating patients is harmful. Drugs all too often cause serious side effects and may sometimes even create new diseases.

(3) "Disease can be cured through the proper use of correct foods. This statement may sound deceptively simple, but I arrived at it only after intensive study of a highly complex subject: colloid and endocrine chemistry."

Dr. Bieler was the first person I read who used the expression "emergency vicarious elimination." My knowledge is extremely limited, yet I'll plunge right in with more "guts" than sense to try to explain this theory at a very elementary level of understanding.

We all know the liver and kidneys are the major eliminative organs of the body. The liver uses the natural avenue of elimination through the bowel; the kidneys, through the bladder and urethra.

However, for too many people the liver is congested and cannot carry on the elimination function properly, so toxins (i.e., waste matter) are pumped into the blood stream. In a similar fashion, the kidneys become overloaded with toxins, which get backed up in the blood. Toxic blood must discharge these waste products, or the person dies. To compensate for this condition, nature uses vicarious/substitute means of elimination. The lungs will take over the job of getting rid of some wastes that the kidneys are supposed to take care of. Or, the skin will help eliminate some liver waste.

Quoting Dr. Bieler, "It stands to reason that the lungs do not make very good kidneys." Resulting irritations, caused by elimination this way, lead to bronchitis, pneumonia, or tuberculosis--depending on individual body chemistry. So the lungs, under duress, pinch-hit for the kidneys. In much the same way, bile poisons in the blood come out through the skin, and we get various irritations of the skin--catarrhs, boils, acne, etc. The skin is substituting for the liver.

So, once again, toxemia is caused by improper foods; elimination becomes an emergency situation; endocrine glands are called into action; alarm, alarm!

The foods we eat today are far removed from what our ancestors ate, yet we still have the same digestive system. If you load up continuously on chili dogs, dinky twinkies, French fries, doughnuts, all washed down with strong coffee or cola, your liver cannot take the insult for too long--even if you're lucky enough to be born with a fine liver.

Sooner or later it will begin to fail: too many additives, pesticides, processed, artificial foods to be filtered and neutralized.

A few words about the endocrine, or ductless, glands of the body are in order. I'm referring to the adrenal, thyroid, and pituitary glands in particular, even though there are others.

The endocrine glands are called into action to aid in eliminating toxic poisons from the system. This is an added line of defense--a back up system, so to speak--that comes into play when the liver is overloaded, doing its job. The endocrines try to direct these excess toxins into other eliminative organs. The major endocrine glands are the pituitary (at the base of the brain), the thyroid (in the neck), and the adrenals (over each kidney).

These glands of internal secretion may be forced to do too much, coerced to make too many of their secretions. The amount of each gland's secretions is in exact ratio to the volume of blood entering it;

therefore, the glands often become enlarged by the extra blood supply, which often has a disastrous physical consequence.

In "reading" my own body, I have found that when I ingest too many sugars and starches that ferment in the intestines I get a migraine headache. The pituitary gland, encased in a bony cup at the base of the skull has swollen from the extra blood in there needed to detoxify my body. The gland pressing against the skull gives me the migraine. If I delete the starches and sugars, the pain goes away.

The last thing I'll mention regarding toxemia and "emergency vicarious elimination" is the belief held by Dr. Bieler that of the contributing factors causing cancer--the hyperactivity of the adrenals may be one of the most important factors to consider.

There's certainly something to think about. Maybe the combination of toxemia and stress (especially emotional distress) causes tissue damage and eventually cancer.

If you're taking any of the following drugs, you need to know the risks involved and the nutritional implications:

DRUG	MECHANISM	NUTRITIONAL IMPLICATION
Analgesics Alcohol	Toxic effect on intestinal mucosa. Impairs pancreatic enzymes ecretion.	Decreased absorption of thiamin, folic acid, vitamin B_{12}. Increased urinary excretion of magnesium and zinc.

Aspirin	Block uptake of vitamin C by platelets.	Decrease serum folate. Increased urinary excretion of vitamin C.
Amphetamines Dextroamphetamine	Decrease appetite.	Decreased caloric intake and possibly reduced growth.
Antacids Alumium hydroxide	Decreases absorption of phosphate.	Phosphate depletion.
Anticonvulsants Phenobarbital Phenytoin Primidone	Increase turnover of vitamin D, may block hydroxylation of vitamin D.	Decreased serum levels of folate, vitamin B_{12}, pyridoxine, 25-hydroxyvitamin D_3 and calcium. Possible osteomalacia.
Barbiturates	Accelerate inactivation of vitamin D.	Decreased absorption of thiamin. Increased urinary excretion of vitamin C. Decreased serum vitamin B_{12}.

Antimicrobials

Penicillin	Carries potassium with it into urine.	Hypokalemis.
Tetracycline	Chelate divalent ions. May decrease synthesis of mucosal ironcarrier protein.	Decreased absorption of calcium, iron, magnesium, xylose, amino acids and fat. Increased urinary excretion of vitamin C, Riboflavin, nitrogen, folic acid & niacin.
Neomycin	Decreases activity of disaccharidases. Causes mucosal injury. Precipatates bile acids and disruptes	Decreased absorption of fat, carbohydrates, protein, fat oluable vit., itamin B12, calcium, iron.
Gathartics	Can cause intestinal hyperperistalsis. May irritate intestine.	Can cause steatorrhea. Can increase intestinal calcium and potassium loss. Decreased glucose absorption.

Vitamin C

Even a partial listing of the benefits of vitamin C is impressive.

Do you want to start an argument? Ask the question, "Does vitamin C have any value in cancer prevention or treatment?" I'll show my cards right from the start: I believe that vitamin C helps prevent cancer and should be used in the treatment of cancer. Please note: I didn't say vitamin C would cure cancer. I don't know of anyone making that claim.

I find "laughable" the number of studies done with *incurable* cancer patients where some researcher used vitamin C, or vitamin A, or some trace element, and announces for the whole world to hear, "Vitamin C won't cure cancer." The most recent study, published in the *New England Journal of Medicine*, was conducted by Dr. Charles Moertel at the Mayo Clinic in Rochester, Minnesota, using one hundred people with incurable colon cancer.

Sadly, I quote: "Our previous study and this one have demonstrated to my satisfaction that vitamin C is worthless in the treatment of advanced and metastatic (spreading) cancer." Dr. Moertel and others have been critical of the research findings of Nobel laureate Dr. Linus Pauling and Dr. Evan Cameron, who reported patients taking vitamin C survived an average of 293 days, while those who didn't take the vitamin C lived thirty-eight days, into the study.

Since nothing else worked with these patients, I wonder if chemotherapy and radiation treatment will get the same press. "Chemotherapy judged worth-

less in the treatment of advanced colon cancer."
Don't hold your breath. You're not likely to see that
day.

Let me expound more regarding the study of Drs.
Evan Cameron and Linus Pauling. In 1971, these
doctors conducted some experiments with more
than one thousand terminally ill cancer patients,
judged hopelessly sick and way beyond any form of
the then available cancer therapy. Vitamin C in large
amounts was given daily to one hundred patients.
All others, the control group, were not dosed. At
the end of this year study, it was found that ninety
percent of the vitamin C-treated patients *lived three
times as long as the untreated patients,* and ten percent of the treated patients lived *twenty* times as long
as the untreated patients.

All of the one thousand control-patients were
dead by 1976. Eighteen of the one hundred vitamin
C-treated patients were still alive, six still living in
1978.

Not only did the patients using vitamin C live
longer, but the quality of their lives was greatly improved. They had less pain, were happier, and were
more productive.

Dr. Cameron believes that malignant cancer may
be caused by the breakdown of collagen, the connective tissue of the body that holds us together (the
"glue" or "cement"). This glue holds our cells in
harness and keeps them from multiplying in a spo-
radic, aimless course. Our cells are enmeshed in the
collagen with cohesion and control. The collagen
can be broken down by an enzyme known as
hyaluronidase. This enzyme is held in check by a
substance called physiological hyaluronidase-in-
hibitors (PHI). PHI needs vitamin C for its production. If vitamin C levels are too low, there may not

be sufficient PHI to stop the destruction of collagen by the enzyme hyaluronidase, and cells become free to proliferate in uncontrolled ways, as in cancer.

Several doctors/scientists have measured blood level vitamin C in hundreds of cancer patients and found them too low in vitamin C. I find it fascinating that x-ray, surgery, chemotherapy, and cobalt treatments all lower patients' vitamin C levels.

Again I feel the need to caution readers that I'm not against chemotherapy, X-ray, or other forms of treatment. I think patients can tolerate those treatments with much less discomfort and less destruction to the body if they ingest large doses of vitamin C and other nutrients. In Japan, intravenous vitamin C often follows intravenous chemotherapy.

There is a current interest in interferon. Professor Benjamin V. Siegel of the University of Oregon Health Services Center in Portland is one of the pioneers in this research. Evidence is accumulating that vitamin C induces the body to produce interferon (i.e., anti-viral substances). One study of mice infected with a leukemia virus showed that large amounts of vitamin C produced twice the interferon of those not receiving ascorbate (i.e., vitamin C).

Dr. Siegel explains the mechanism by which interferon works this way: Interferon increases the activity of macrophages, large white blood cells that devour and destroy the harmful cells of a virus or cancer. Vitamin C also activates white cells from the thymus gland, often referred to as T-cells. Virus and/or cancer cells contact T-cells, which become sensitized and then release hormones (lymphokines), in turn, activating more macrophages. Thus, relatively few T-cells can lead to the stimulation of large numbers of macrophages. (Some studies have shown that cancer patients in general are too low in

T-cell counts). In broad terms, this is how the body's immune system works. The encasing and dissolving of "enemy" cells is called phagocytosis; T-cells may be thought of as a sort of vigilante squad patrolling the body and prepared to signal the process of phagocytosis to get going.

I think Dr. Siegel could plead a good case in favor of megadoses of vitamin C.

Doctors Pauling and Cameron, when asked if vitamin C treatment should be standard procedure in cancer treatment, replied: "Supplemental ascorbate is of some value to *all* cancer patients and can be of dramatic benefit to a fortunate few."

Controversy continues to circulate regarding the importance of daily vitamin C intake way beyond that recommended by established authorities, despite the fact that double-bind studies support these findings of Doctors Pauling and Cameron.

To those who will listen, Dr. Richard Passwater points out that man no longer lives in a "natural environment" like his descendants and that his body now has to cope with a variety of unnatural factors (i.e., chemical pollutants, radiation, carcinogens we don't even know about yet). So, Dr. Passwater suggests we may be better protected and benefit from "unnaturally" large supplements of vitamins, minerals, and nutrients, especially antioxidants like vitamins C and E.

A few short years ago I read a review of Public Broadcasting System television special about cancer in China. What captured my interest the most was that one out of four people in the Lin Xian area was dying of esophageal cancer. I watched the program, open-mouthed in wonder. The following is a brief account of that show:

The Lin Xian area has the highest esophageal cancer statistics in the world and, additionally, one of the worst overall cancer rates. In one commune alone it was established that the fourteen thousand chickens in the area had the same incidence of esophageal cancer as the people. As Alice said in Wonderland, "Things are getting curiouser and curiouser."

The Cancer Research Institute in Peking, China, was assigned the responsibility to "find out what's causing this cancer and stop it." A team was sent in, made up of all kinds of specialists: virologists, pathologists, surgeons, endocrinologists, biochemists, oncologists, nutritionists, and more.

One hundred thousand people were involved in the research project, using an interdisciplinarian approach, with the major emphasis on prevention and education. Some workers were identified as "street doctors", others as "workers doctors", and a third category, as "barefoot doctors."

The research team conducted an exhaustive study, examining possible causes, chemical and non-chemical (radiation). They looked at patterns of behavior as well as internal conditions that might prevent the body from calling up its own immunization system.

In the Lin Xian area, the main source of food was ground-up turnips, cabbage, and grains. The crops were harvested, soaked in water, cut up, mashed, and rolled into patties, then smoked in primitive ovens until the patties are brick-hard. Because of the lack of electricity and refrigeration, the patties are lined upon the outside roof and taken down, as needed, for consumption.

When the natives cracked open one of the patties, they would feed the crumbs to the chickens. The plot thickens.

The local water supply was deficient in the trace

element maliganum and very high in nitrate content. Subjected to temperature extremes, nitrates and nitrites change into nitrosamines. Nitrosamines are among the world's most deadly cancer-causing substances. When the natives baked and smoked their patties, after soaking them in nitrate-loaded water, they turned the nitrates into nitrosamines; ergo, cancer ran rampant.

Guess where you get nitrates and nitrites almost every day? You get them in fruits and vegetables soaked in nitrites to keep them fresh looking; in most cold cuts; in bacon, sausages, and other meats that use nitrates to preserve the meats and keep them fresh-looking. And what do you do with those meats when you get them home? You very likely either freeze them or cook them, turning the nitrates/nitrites into nitrosamines. Tragic!

Back to Lin Xian. The Cancer Research team found blood sample levels of vitamin C were extremely low in the population. They took hundreds of urine samples and tested for nitrate content. The team then gave each subject one thousand milligrams of vitamin C, and the next day took another urine sample. After one ingestion of the vitamin C, the nitrate content of the urine was cut by one third.

The Food and Drug Administration has considered, for some time, ordering the addition of vitamin C to all meats treated with nitrites. Sounds promising. But why doesn't the FDA have the meat processing industry cut out the nitrites/nitrates? How would food look fresh or be preserved?

The Chinese, great believers in herbs, have used many for medicinal purposes for thousands of years. They used a kind of preventive chemotherapy: vitamin B3 mixed with certain herbs were found to have an anti-tumor effect and to draw out fever temperatures in other tumors.

The last thing the Chinese did was to resettle fifty thousand people from the Lin Xian area to another part of China. After a couple of years of relocation, only twelve more cancer patients were recorded.

There hasn't been an antibiotic yet invented that can do for you what vitamin C can do for you. The following is a partial list of benefits from vitamin C:

1. Regulates amino acid metabolism.
2. Helps build collagen, the connective tissue of the body.
3. Detoxifies poisons and pollutants we ingest.
4. Promotes the absorption of copper and iron.
5. Stimulates the adrenals--part of your body's immunization system.
6. Plays a major role in regulating stress.
7. Helps the body heal wounds.
8. Stimulates white blood cell production.
9. Discourages the conversion of nitrites and nitrates into carcinogenic nitrosamines.
10. Acts as a coenxzyme essential in producing collagen, pigment molecules, steroid hormones.
11. Reduces vulnerability to disease and infection.
12. Promotes strong bones, teeth, gums, and healthy skin.

Do you still want to settle for forty milligrams as your RDA? No way. Not this guy. Eighty percent of vitamin C is lost in the commercial blanching, sterilizing, and soaking process of canning fresh garden peas. Sixty percent is lost when freezing them. Typical cooking will reduce vitamin C by fifty percent, and so on. The same losses apply to other fruits and vegetables. Of course, if you smoke, drink alcoholic beverages, or both you're at great risk because those deadly habits deplete your body of vitamin C and other essential nutrients. Each cigarette smoked destroys about twenty-five to thirty milligrams of vitamin C.

When people get headaches and feel "stressed out," they often take aspirin. Too much aspirin is bad for you and will enhance the negative aspects of stress. Also, the aspirin can promote ulcers by irritating the stomach lining and can actually force vitamin C out of your body, setting up a negative cyclical effect. Lack of vitamin C slows down your body's ability to excrete aspirin.

One myth regarding vitamin C is perpetuated; namely, that vitamin C causes kidney stones and destroys vitamin B_{12}. One doctor wrote an article in the New England Journal of Medicine about twenty-five years ago stating this "truth." We now know that vitamin C helps prevent kidney stones and does not affect vitamin B_{12}. The medical journals have yet to print this updated information; such is the politics of medicine.

SELENIUM

Over thirty scientific papers show hard evidence that selenium in the diet can inhibit or postpone the development of cancer in laboratory animals and probably humans.

I consider the remarkable mineral selenium of equal importance to the information I already shared with you readers regarding the thymus gland. Do yourself a great service and read Dr. Richard A. Passwater's book, *Selenium As Food and Medicine.* He and others present a convincing compendium showing that selenium deficiency is associated with heart disease, cancer, premature aging, and other afflictions.

Scientists from around the world assembled in the spring of 1980 at the Texas Tech University in Lubbock, Texas, to discuss ideas and research in selenium's role in preventing diseases. This was the Second International Symposium on Selenium in Biology and Medicine. The facts about selenium are well known in this small scientific fraternity; however, the general lay public knows very little about selenium.

About twenty-five years ago, Klaus Schwarz, M.D., and his colleagues established the critical need in human nutrition of certain trace elements; namely, selenium, chromium and fluorine. Dr. Schwarz has died, and the mantle has been given over to Dr. Passwater.

Mrs. Joyce Ann Schwarz, widow of Dr. Schwarz, says, "Rarely has a book been written with a greater potential for improving the health and welfare of people around the globe." I don't think this is an exaggeration.

Dr. Passwater's book is brimful of "population studies, clinical studies and laboratory experiments that establish without a doubt selenium's vital role in the prevention of heart disease and many forms of cancer."

Our bodies are made up of about sixty trillion cells, and every day those cells require selenium to protect their membranes.

Dr. Passwater and other selenium researchers believe that improved selenium nutrition can reduce the risk of cancer. In numerous studies, minimal amounts of selenium were added to the usual diets of animals who had been injected with cancer-causing substances. "In almost every case, *selenium* supplementation substantially reduced the incidence of cancer."

There is impressive evidence that increased selenium intake can and does protect people as well. Regional and population studies have been consistent: Insufficient amounts of selenium in different states and areas of the United States may contribute to the increased incidences of breast, colon, ovary, pancreas, prostrate, lung, and bladder cancer in those regions.

Selenium is a naturally occurring trace element. Comparative studies of lung cancer in various countries throughout the world produced some fascinating food for thought. In countries where tobacco is grown in selenium deficient soil, there are higher incidences of lung cancer than in those countries where the selenium count in the soil is high.

After my second bout with cancer I read an article about insufficient blood level selenium counts in eighty-five percent of the cancer patients tested. There wasn't much of an explanation, but it was enough to convince me to increase my selenium intake. A number of physicians found that when they had cancer patients raise their selenium blood levels their tumors began to shrink.

It seems to me, based on extensive library research, that there's no valid scientific reason to doubt that selenium protects us against many types of cancer. Literally dozens of very carefully controlled, scientific studies have been done in several countries, which all came to the same conclusion: *Selenium deficiency can interfere with cancer cure.*

Even more studies have been conducted in cardiovascular diseases and selenium. Many of them suggest that selenium is an important protective factor in high blood pressure, stroke, heart attack, and hypertensive kidney damage. As with cancer, people living in areas low in selenium content in the soil have high rates of heart disease, while those inhabitants with high selenium intake have low rates of heart disease.

However, it must be pointed out that soil content is only part of the problem. Regions of the United States where selenium is present are being depleted by some fertilization practices, high levels of sulfate in the air from burning oil and coal, and acid rain.

The National Research Council suggests a daily intake of fifty to two hundred micrograms (please note, I said "micrograms" and not "milligrams") daily. Most Americans ingest between thirty to sixty micrograms per day. Based on the information I've gathered on this subject, I would opt for between 250 and 350 micrograms a day. Additionally I think that women, especially if they have breast cancer in the family history, should get about three hundred micrograms per day.

Each year there are about 100,000 new cases of

breast cancer in America. Dr. Daniel Medina, at the Baylor College of Medicine in Houston, has success- fully used selenium against breast tumors in his labo- ratory animals. Selenium can inhibit in the early stages the development of tumors that were induced by viral or chemical carcinogens. The mechanism of how it works is still being investigated.

There have been over thirty scientific papers showing hard evidence that selenium in the diet can inhibit or postpone the development of cancer in laboratory animals and probably humans. I don't have to wait around for more confirming evidence.

Another study done recently at Roswell Park Memorial Institute in Buffalo, New York, showed that a blend of selenium and vitamin A reduced by more than ninety percent the number of tumors in rats. Dr. Clement Ip was the principal researcher in these studies.

Some scientists theorize that selenium somehow protects deoxyribonucleic acid (DNA) molecules from damage and encourages their repair. So far this theory is inconclusive. Other researchers think the most important contribution takes place in the liver, where selenium may block the conversion of certain chemicals into carcinogens.

Eat more fish and less processed meats. Nuts, whole wheat bread, and vegetables grown in seleni- um rich soil are good sources of selenium in our di- ets.

At this point in time no one is saying--at least to my knowledge--that selenium will cure cancer. However, it is becoming increasingly clear that sele- nium deficiency does interfere with a cancer cure.

I would urge any cancer patient to increase his blood level of selenium in conjunction with his can- cer treatment--no matter what that treatment is.

In 1967 the United States Department of Agriculture (USDA) made a map of the United States showing by color key what the selenium content of soil was in different areas. The USDA used three colors to denote the concentrations of "low", "variable or medium", and "adequate."

Dr. Gerhard Schrauzer made a map of the United States indicating the incidences and concentrations of cancer in the various States. The correlations between the USDA and Dr. Schrauzer's map is enlightening. There's an almost perfect correlation: the States with the lowest selenium content are among the States with the highest cancer rates. The States with the most selenium have significantly lower cancer rates.

"No matter how well food is selected, if there isn't any selenium in the soil there can't be any in the crops or livestock."

At a conference of the International Association of Bioinorganic Scientists, held in San Diego, California, January, 1979, some of the world's leading nutritional scientists said they believe there is sufficient evidence that selenium can reduce some cancers and that a national trial should be conducted on humans. "A supplementation of the diet with 100 to 200 micrograms of selenium will reduce the occurrence of some cancers in humans."

Dr. Gerhard Schrauzer of the University of California, San Diego, reported to the Workshop of Chemoprevention of Cancer at the National Cancer Institute in Bethesda, Maryland, that "The key to cancer prevention lies in assuring the adequate intake of selenium, as well as other essential trace elements."

Dr. Douglas Frost, former researcher at Dartmouth Medical School's Trace Element Laboratory, puts it rather succinctly: "There is damn good evidence that selenium has anti-cancer value. If we want to avoid getting cancer, we should be sure to get enough selenium."

Dr. Charles Shaw of the M. D. Auderson Hospital and Tumor Institute in Houston, Texas, who has reduced cancer in laboratory animals, states with scientific conservatism: "There seems to be a causal relationship between having high selenium levels and not having cancer. It all fits a common picture."

All of the research on selenium incorporated epidemiological studies, laboratory experiments and clinical observations. Based an epidemiological studies, Dr. Raymond Shamberger of the Cleveland Clinic Foundation, advises people to increase their intake of selenium to two hundred micrograms a day, because "It can reduce the cancer rate dramatically for some types of cancer, particularly cancer of the colon, breast, esophagus, tongue, stomach, intestine, rectum, and bladder."

Study after study, too numerous to expound on in this book, come to the same conclusions: To help *prevent* cancer, increase your selenium intake. To *aid* in the cure of cancer, supplement your diet with greater amounts of selenium.

Selenium protects your cell membranes, stimulates your body's immune response, safeguards your liver, detoxifies your body from environmental carcinogens and radiation, and other beneficial body guards too technical for me to discuss on a layman's level.

In every resource on the subject I looked at, blood selenium levels are directly related to survival time of cancer patients. More selenium, longer the survival time. Less selenium, shorter time; more recurrences of cancer and metastasis.

The last thing I will mention regarding selenium is the wealth of knowledge accumulated that selenium not only protects against cancer and heart disease, but that it also slows the aging process. (I know...sounds like a "snake oil" salesman).

Please don't misunderstand what I'm saying here. There is *no* implication that ingesting extra selenium will make you younger. It will not. However, research shows that if you fail to get your optimum amount of selenium, you get older before your time. Your body will not have full protection against aging factors and you will look older and physiologically be older than you would be otherwise.

It really makes a lot of sense to me that if you can slow down the aging process, you're also protecting yourself from disease. There is a strong correlation between most types of cancer and age. The aging process probably makes people more vulnerable to cancer and other degenerative diseases.

Dr. Passwater says, "Selenium is not a panacea. It doesn't promise to cure whatever ails you." More research is needed to shed light on selenium's role in health.

While some of you wait for more scientific validation, I'm going to take my three hundred micrograms of selenium every day.

To your health!

CANCER and EXERCISE

Exercise has more than physical benefits; it can produce significant psychological changes as well.

Make exercise a habit! You'll find that regular, vigorous exercise can work wonders for your body. But keep it fun!

We have all heard about the manifold benefits of exercise. It increases heart, lung, and muscle efficiency, slows down the effects of aging, keeps weight under control, provides more energy for daily tasks, and generally makes you feel better. It also improves posture, balance, and coordination as well as the reduction and relief of stress and fatigue. Besides, there is an increase in endurance and stamina and joint mobility.

Also, there is some evidence that certain cancer cells cannot tolerate oxygen. As a cancer patient, that suggests very strongly to me how important it is to get a lot of oxygen pumping through my body. The combination of exercise, niacin, and vitamin E (which increases the efficiency of your lungs in the exchange of oxygen and carbon dioxide) provides lots of oxygen. Further, fat cells in your body store toxic wastes. Exercise burns off calories and helps rid your body of toxic substances.

As I've already mentioned, and it's worth reinforcing, I believe your energy level is one of the most important signs of vibrant health, and conversely, the lack of energy, an indication of un-wellness. Scientists have discovered that light exercise is better than passive resting for exhaustion. So, if you opt for a strenuous exercise program, which may cause fatigue, "active rest" is more beneficial to refill your energy reserves. Don't flop down, do nothing, and suck on a beer in front of the TV set. You have to remove the waste products of fatigue, i.e., fatigue metabolites, such as lactic acid salts. Active rest speeds up the recovery process. An important paradox to keep in mind is that the human body must be used in order to save itself. Although mechanical engines wear out with use, eventually, the human body improves with use.

Much data suggest that, generally speaking, as people reach their middle years, they are more apt to become addicted to medications, food, and alcohol. (Usually it takes between 15-25 years to produce a chronic-addictive alcoholic.) During the years when the paunch begins, people normally suffer from health problems that are associated with high tension or distress. These middle-aged people are encountering more stress and experiencing more depression. This, too, opens them up to the onset of disease. Remember, my first bout with cancer was when I was 43 years old.

Since stress cannot be avoided, it is important to note that well-conditioned people naturally control those common reactions to stress better than the people who are unfit. There are sufficient scientific data to back up this hypothesis. Exercises usually handle stress better than their sedentary counterparts.

Some cancer researchers will tell you that cancer is much more likely to occur in the wealthy and lazy man than in the economically poor, hardworking man. Cancer does appear to be a product of the Machine Age.

Many animal studies support the idea that the more muscular effort you exert, the less cancer is likely to occur. Research has been done comparing mice given an unrestricted diet and very little exercise. The mice with uncontrolled eating and no exercise had a cancer rate of 88 percent compared to 16 percent for the other group. Similar studies showed decreased tumor growth in laboratory animals that were exercised.

One of the best resources I came across on cancer and exercise is provided in the book *Getting Well Again.*

In one ingenious study reported in 1960, S. Hoffman and K. Paschkis took an extract from fatigued (exercised) muscle tissues of mice and injected it into mice in which they had also transplanted cancerous cells. They discovered that the muscle tissue extract led to decreased tumor growth and, in a few cases, to disappearance of malignancy. An injection of extract from nonfatigued muscle had no effect.

The work of Dr. Hans Selye and other stress researchers suggests that the correspondence between exercise and reduced incidence of cancer may be related to the appropriate channeling of stress. A number of animal studies have shown that when animals are stressed again and again and not permitted a physical outlet for releasing the stress, there is a steady deterioration of their bodies. But if animals are stressed and then allowed to physically act, the amount of damage is minimal.

These findings are supported by data from other animal experiments. Here again, it has been shown that vigorous exercise seems to stimulate the immune system and reverse the physiological effects of stress. Does all this information garnered from animal experiments apply to human beings? I'm not going to wait for more research. I'm putting on my sweats and heading for the gym.

Besides physical benefits, exercise effects important psychological changes as well as an increased sense of self-acceptance, more flexibility, tolerance, and less depression. All in all, this leads to a healthier psychological profile, a strong component in staying and getting well. Setting time aside for regular exercise means taking control of your life and making a positive emotional statement. For there seems to be a correlation between depression and the beginning or prolongation of disease.

I've heard all the common excuses for not exercising. They range from expense through boredom to self-consciousness. But something as simple as a brisk walk is incomparable exercise, and it costs nothing. Mixing up your exercises prevents boredom. And we've all disguised our figure faults with larger-sized clothing--so, do the same with exercise garb.

The excuses I hear most often are: "There's no time" and "I'm bushed". The truth of the matter is you can make time. A little self-discipline will easily free up twenty minutes three times a week. And I promise you, exercising will pick you up, energizing your body and lifting your spirit. That is because exercising releases endorphins, a body chemistry similar to morphine, that makes you feel good about yourself. The release of these endorphins, which act as antidepressants, is better than any drug prescription you can find.

If you become involved in a formal, public exercise program, I caution you: first, be certain you join a program designed by directors knowledgeable about human physiology. Too many money-making exercise programs are misleading--all glitz and no substance--leading even to physical injury. Second, be certain to find a program that is fun. Otherwise, you are adding more stress to your life and the exercise program will be counter-productive.

What if you are bedridden? Is there some way you can tie into the benefits of exercising? It has been suggested that our physical limitations can be overcome by a combination of light movement and mental imagery. You are told to raise and lower your arms or legs gently for four to five minutes. Next, you are told to visualize yourself engaging in taxing physical exercise...like playing tennis or walking at a good pace along the shore for five or ten minutes. Then go into visualizing yourself exercising again for five to ten minutes.

Evidence continues to mount. Exercise is beneficial to body and mind. It stimulates the immune system. It lifts depression. It leads to greater energy and to sustained health. You can find an exercise program that fits you. It's worth trying out a few to find one or a mix that suits you...and is fun. The body and mind are inseparable, and the body-mind rewards from exercise are incalculable.

THYMUS

The more we can stimulate thymus activity through-out life the greater will be our ability to ward off cancer.

One time I was asked, "What do you think was the single, most important health tip you learned in your cancer fight?" That's an impossible question for me to answer. However, I could narrow the answer down to a few subjects. (By the way, the question reveals to me the prevalent belief that one specific cause can be blamed for cancer, or any disease, so one specific cure must be the answer).

In this chapter I want to share with you readers *one* of the most portentous, exciting morsels of information you can use in your daily life. I found this enlightenment in a paperback book, entitled *Your Body Doesn't Lie*, by John Diamond, M.D. Dr. Diamond's book was one of the main selections suggested one month by the *Psychology Today* Book Club.

The primary focus of Dr. Diamond's book is the thymus gland, a little known, under appreciated, almost magical, tiny organ of the body.

For several years, on an intuitive level, one of the best indicators I used to judge the progress, or lack thereof, of cancer patients was their energy level. When I perceived their energy slipping, this indicated to me that prognosis was going poorly. On the other hand, when patients reported large energy reserves, I knew they were "winning." Diamond's book answered all my questions regarding people's energy source.

Count down a couple of ribs; trace the rib over

to your breast bone; just beneath the upper part of that sternum lies the thymus. It is present in all mammals and could be covered by an object as small as a silver dollar.

Please understand the importance of the following: under stress, acute stress, such as infection, diagnosis of illness, and prolonged stress, such as chronic illness, divorce, etc., the thymus can shrivel up, atrophy to half its size in twenty-four hours. This ever so critical guardian of your health; this seat of your energy and T-cell production; this first line of defense can be knocked out in very little time when it is most needed. I ask you readers, who is under more stress than a recently diagnosed cancer patient and his/her kin and loving friends?

Literally dozens of experiments have proven that when the thymus is removed or destroyed, or its effectiveness diminished, the immune system of the body breaks down and is opened to infection and cancerous growth. If the thymus is strong and intact, tumors will be recognized as hostile invaders and attacked.

There are a number of ways to protect and strengthen the thymus, as there are dozens to weaken it. A lot of evidence has been accumulated that enhancement of the immune response is possible-- more accurately, I should say likely--by the ingestion of thymus extract and may help overcome some forms of cancer.

Diamond reminds us that as far back as 1902, a Dr. Faulerton in London, was using thymus extract in the treatment of cancer with favorable results.

Behavioral kinesiologists believe that every major muscle of the body relates to an organ within that body. If a muscle tests weak, then the corresponding organ is not functioning to its full capacity.

It's almost embarrassing for me to explain the rewards I've gained from Diamond's book. My energy level is astounding to most people. Those that know I'm fifty-five years old and routinely work nine- and ten-hour days find it hard to believe. I ride a bike between ten to eleven kilometers in less than twenty minutes three times a week. My workouts at the health club put most of the teenagers and twenty-year-olds to shame. In my teaching, counseling, and in my personal acquaintances, I energize others--and show them how to energize themselves. The application of this knowledge seem limitless to me. However, I must quickly add, what was esoteric knowledge is becoming widely known by those professionals involved in the relatively new science and philosophy, called "Behavioral Kinesiology." Behavioral Kinesiology incorporates all the healing arts from psychosomatic medicine, sports training, allergy, nutrition, dentistry, and others.

Dr. Diamond says, "I have come to believe that all illness starts as a problem on the *energy* level, a problem that may exist for many years before it manifests itself in physical disease. It appears that a generalized reduction of body energy leads to energy imbalances in particular parts of the body. If we become aware of these energy imbalances when they first occur, we have a long grace period in which to correct them. We will then be practicing primary prevention."

I believe that one of the most important goals in any therapeutic modality is to give clients a greater sense of their own power, abilities, capacities, what have you. It's incredibly invigorating just to accept responsibility for your self--for the way you behave, feel, and react. I encourage my students to learn the skills necessary to give back to their clients this power, this responsibility for well-being. Teaching and therapy are shared responsibilities. Validate others; however, they must learn to self-validate as well. They have the inner ability--and can gain knowledge--to mobilize toward health.

Dr. Carl Simonton was the first person I ever heard talk about T-cells. All I knew about them was that they were white blood cells important in fighting off microscopic body invaders. Most cancer patients are deficient in T-cell counts. By the way, the "T" stands for thymus derived.

How does it work? I'm not exactly sure. At the present time, our knowledge is still somewhat limited but a "golden age of thymology" is beginning.*

Diamond, Nossal and others refer to the thymus as the "school and factory" for lymphocytes--the white blood cells responsible for the immunological reactions in the body. Immature lymphoctyes come to the thymus from the bone marrow. They develop under influence of the thymus hormones, leave the thymus and settle in the lymph nodes and spleen, where they give rise to other generations of lymphocytes called T-cells. Thymus hormones continuously travel throughout the bloodstream and exert their influence over the departed T-cells.

The thymus hormones are used in growth and development of the human body; however, after puberty the thymus is smaller because it's no longer concerned with growth. Further shrinkage is due to stress and other factors.

The thymus prepares the T-cell to do its work-- identify friend from foe, and destroy foreign cells. This role, called "immunological surveillance," is directly concerned with resistance to infections and cancer.

According to the surveillance theory, everyone

produces abnormal cells in the body from time to time. Normally, the body's immune system, especially T-cells, keeps a close watch out for these strange cells and eradicates them. That's why the term "surveillance" is used. For cancer to occur, then, the immune system must be weakened/inhibited in some way. One way is the suppression or extinguishing of the thymus gland's job. Weaken the thymus and a domino effect takes place throughout the body's natural immunization defense system.

Probably the most acceptable theory of cancer is that formulated by Sir MacFarlane Burnet, "the Australian Nobel Prize winner. Of the billions of new cells produced in the body each day, some will be abnormal. One of the functions of the T-cells is to recognize these abnormal cells are not activated by the thymus hormone, the abnormal cells may "take" and develop into clinical cancer. Hence the critical role of the thymus gland throughout adult life in the prevention of cancer.

Now we begin to understand why cancer increases with age. It has been shown that the antibody response of old mice is only about five percent that of young mice. Old mice cannot reject cancer cells injected into them. However, if old mice are given thymus hormone at the same time, cancer does not develop. In all mammalian species there is a falling off in thymus activity with advancing years, and a corresponding increase in the rate of cancer. The more we can stimulate thymus activity throughout life, the greater will be our ability to ward off cancer.

The dramatic atrophy of the thymus gland in a person undergoing stress is not fully understood. Within a day of severe injury or sudden illness, millions of lymphocytes are destroyed and the thymus shrinks to half its size. This is part of the general reaction to stress described by Hans Selye.

For the sake of brevity, I can't go into every known condition that will either weaken or strengthen the thymus, thereby raising or lowering your energy level and body strength. The following are some considerations that are quantitative and have been tested by Behavioral Kinesiology specialists:

1. Stress and cerebral balance.,
2. Your emotions--positive ones strengthen your thymus; negative emotions weaken your thymus.
3. The people around you.
4. Your physical environment. Too numerous to mention them all. Things like sunglasses, artificial or synthetic fabrics, high-heeled shoes, toiletries, certain metals, lighting, household fuels, smoking, automobile exhaust fumes, sound waves, etc., all may devitalize your body.
5. Certain kinds and pieces of music.
6. Food.
7. Posture.

Dr. Ott researched the relationship between some artificial lighting and illness. There is a negative effect on the function of the endrocrine system, certain nervous disorders, and maybe even cancer.

Dr. Ott thinks that "the predominance of all kinds of artificial lighting is closely related to modern illness, chronic fatigue, and imbalances on many levels of our being."

One day while sitting in the library at Springfield College I felt my energy draining from my body. I became very weak, very fast. I looked around my immediate environment and focused on the fluorescent lamp next to my head. At that moment one of my students walked by and I asked him to test my thymus for me. I moved away from the lamp and my thymus tested strong. I went over and sat under the light for a second and my thymus tested weak. That damned light was sapping my energy.

THERAPEUTIC TOUCH

God gave us a wonderful gift through which we may channel the love and concern in our hearts. That gift is our hands. We can learn to use them to relieve suffering, express affection, and communicate involvement.

We all have this marvelous ability to assist people, to relieve pain, and to promote healing. We can do this with a very simple act: reach out and touch others in a nurturing, affectional way, transmitting some of our own energy to them. There are currents of life-force, a subtle form of electromagnetic energy, that flow naturally through our hands. Because the electromagnetic field extends beyond our bodies, we can release and balance another person's energy. When energy flows freely, there is an experience of peace and joy.

Those magnetic fields have been investigated. Scientific experiments illustrate the use of these magnetic fields to move quartz crystals without discernible physical contact. Also, it has been shown that measurable changes take place in body chemistry just by concentrating our attention. Thus, we don't even have to touch someone to "touch" him. We can touch people just by our intentions.

It is known that I have worked with murderers, rapists, armed robbers, drug pushers, child molesters, and wife beaters. So, I have been asked on several occasions if I'm ever physically afraid of counselling potentially violent clients. My response is the same as that Jerry Jampolski gave when asked this very question: "I'm never afraid because somehow or other I communicate my intentionality." My clients, "touched" by my good intentions, know I mean them no harm. I only want to help them: therefore, they perceive I am no threat.

I served in the United States Army in 1954-55 and was stationed in Boblingen, Germany, just outside Stuttgart. My wife and I considered adopting a racially mixed child--the father, a black American G.I.; the mother, a white German. We visited a couple of places where a Catholic order of nuns took care of these "throw-away" infants. It was the only time I'd ever seen a mirasmus child. From my limited knowledge, the child seemed emotionally dead. In other words, the will to live, the thrust toward life, never got turned on. This tragic child just lay in his crib: He wouldn't respond to tactile or visual stimuli; he was cold and clammy to the touch; he didn't cry or smile, his eyes, expressionless, dull, open but not seeing. The kindly nuns had found him too late to save him. He died soon after we saw him, and June and I waited until we returned to the United States to continue our search for adoptable children.

Our first adopted child was Keith. He was four weeks old when June and I picked him up at the Diocesan Bureau in Hartford, Connecticut. Talk about a peak experience. I could hardly contain my excitement while driving home. June sat holding the baby in her arms with tears of gladness streaming down her face. I wanted to stop the car, get out, and run--run like the wind, run for the sheer exhilaration of running, run to express the explosion of joy in me.

Several years later I did some training at the Moreno Institute of Psychodrama where I elected to be the protagonist in a psychodrama reliving one of the happiest moments in my life. I chose to relive the experience of driving home with my first child. In the psychodrama I added what was missing for me in the original experience. I ran and ran and ran all over the Psychodrama theater: around the stage, up the stairs, over the balcony, up and down the aisles, tears of joy pouring down my face. My God, how wonderful it felt to fully express the exhilaration of the happiest moment in my life.

When Keith was a year old he weighed thirty-three pounds. He was big and beautiful. When people asked how he grew so big so fast, I was reminded of the lyrics to a charming song from the musical *Fanny.*

When the baby arrived he weighed eight pounds.
Now he weighs twenty-three.
What are they made of those extra pounds;
    what can they be?
Fifteen pounds of love they are,
Fifteen solid pounds.
Fifteen pounds of caring and sharing and love.
Love is a very light thing.
Love is so fragile and frail.
You can not hold it here in your hand,
Or weigh it on a scale.
Cigarette smoke, that's all it is,
Wispy and curling around.
Oh, it takes a lot of love to make a pound.
Love is a very light thing;,
    light as a song in the air.
How do you start to fill up a heart,
    how many ounces there?
Dragon fly wings, that's all it is,
    whispering by with no sound.
Oh, it takes a lot of love to make a pound.

* * *

As number 11 of 12 children, I figured out at an

early age that the way I could have all of my mother's attention was to get sick. There were lots of "payoffs" in being ill. My mother would drop everything and her first priority was my needs and wants. She would hold and comfort me. Her touch was magical.

Years later, my daughter Jennifer and I were standing in line at a department store counter waiting for service. The young woman at the cash register suddenly stopped moving, became absolutely still, her face transfixed. She was probably having a mild epileptic seizure. I reached out and took the woman's hand in mine. She regained her composure and meekly smiled at me. I reassured her that everything was all right, and she carried on her work. I learned a long time ago that the quickest and easiest method to bring a patient back into the now, the present, is simply to make physical contact.

Dr. Hans Manksch wrote a chapter in Elisabeth Kubler-Ross's book, *Death, the Final Stage of Growth*, entitled, "The Organization Context of Dying." Dr. Manksch addresses several concerns in the hospital setting where too much depersonalization of patients is taking place. He describes patient responses to authority figures and professional attitudes and behaviors, both beneficial and harmful. Dr. Manksch says clearly that making a patient wait too long is punishment and anticipating patients' needs is rewarding. Among medical professionals, behaving as if they don't understand what the patient wants is punishment. Among physicians, taking time to sit down in the patient's room is rewarding.

Dr. Manksch conducted an experiment wherein he asked several physicians to come individually into a patient's room where he would time the length of their stay. The physicians had been asked to remain in the patient's room for exactly three minutes. Four doctors took part in this exercise. With half the patients, they sat down randomly, and with the other half, they remained standing, away from the bed. Dr. Manksch then interviewed the patients. In every instance where the physicians had sat down, the patient believed the doctor had stayed at least ten minutes?

I teach my students to step out of their official roles and away from their professional skills. Touching a patient in one's professional capacity, such as changing a dressing, making a bed, or performing physical or occupational therapy, is really quite different from placing a hand on someone's shoulder gently massaging a sore, tired limb, or sometimes even giving a hug.

I shall never forget visiting my wife in the hospital after she had a breast tumor removed. (It was about a year after I got cancer.) Fortunately, June's tumor was benign, but we didn't know that going into surgery. Both June and I were scared. She was just coming out of the anesthesia. Sitting at the foot of her bed was our pediatrician friend, Dr. Arnold Blake. He was gently and lovingly giving June a foot massage, and she was smiling through her drug-induced bewilderment. My wife is an attractive woman; it is easy for those who love her to touch her. However, I cannot help but think of the hundreds of children and adults I've worked with who are unattractive, sometimes dirty, often deformed, maybe antisocial in behavior. Who is willing to touch them? Yet, who needs it more?

I tell my students who find it difficult to touch other people and to be touched in return not to go into the human-helping professions, at least not as a line, or face-to-face, worker with clients. Instead, I advise them to become an administrator and stay in insulated offices, behind desks.

One of the main reasons so many of us avoid any talk of death is the terrifying, unbearable feeling that there is nothing we can say to comfort our loved ones and friends in such agony. But there is consoling action we can take. Touch them!

I never wonder how to behave when I go to a funeral, visit a loved one in the hospital, or receive a call for help from someone in pain. I simply touch them. I used to worry about what to say to these people who were in the depths of despair. The answer is extremely simple: touch them!

I was present during critical stages in the deaths of two teenagers. When I was called for a consultation, both youngsters, who were dying of cancer, had lots of unfinished business in their short lives. One wanted to talk about death; the other, did not. I simply listened when either wanted to talk, but mostly, we communicated through touch.

Especially in regard to old people, the infirm, the sick, many tend not to touch them when it is needed. If you want to communicate hope, but because of your fears you communicate despair, don't talk. Touch ... and listen, of course.

In the February 1970 issue of *The American Journal of Nursing*, a dying student nurse wrote to her fellow nurses:

"If only we could be honest, both admit of our fears, touch one another. If you really care, would you lose so much of your valuable professionalism if you cried with me? Just person to person? Then, it might not be so hard to die--in a hospital--with friends close."

In the mid 1970s, a study was conducted by nurses at New York University regarding the effects of laying hands on patients. The research, carried on under the direction of nurse-professor Dolores Krieger, reinforced the belief that there is a natural power of life in loving people that is communicated in a special way through the power of touch. Patients absorb this energy while their sick bodies build up their own life energy sources.

Professor Krieger, in *The American Journal of Nursing*, May 1975, page 784, further addresses the *intention of healing*. She conducted several studies on patients, using hemoglobin value of their blood to check what was happening through the laying on of hands. Her studies show that there is a natural power in the laying on of hands, provided (1) the nurse intends to help heal another person, and (2) the nurse is physically healthy herself. Professor Krieger goes on to say on page 786, "I'm convinced that the practice of therapeutic touch is a natural potential in physically healthy persons who are strongly motivated to help ill people, and that this potential can be actualized."

I caution my students about the judicious use of touch in their professional lives. We all come into the world needing to be touched, and it remains a life-long need. Most of us know that being touched in tender ways helps healing. Regrettably, the danger for the professional who works in human services is that for many people there is confusion between a comforting and caring touch and one intended to generate sexual arousal. Also, we need to understand cultural differences in touching.

Science and medicine believe in a general embryological law: the earlier a function develops in the embryo, the more fundamental it is likely to be. A human embryo, less than one inch long from end to end, and less than six weeks old, will bend its neck and trunk if lightly touched. At this stage of development, the fetus has no eyes and no ears, yet its skin is already highly developed.

There is some difference of opinion as to which of our senses is the first one developed. I believe the sense of touch is the first to come into being and, after the brain, the skin is the most important of all organ systems. A piece of skin, no larger than the size of a quarter, contains three million cells, 100 sweat glands, 50 nerve endings, three feet of blood vessels, and 50 receptors for every 100 square millimeters, totaling 640,000 sensory receptors.

A priest once said to me, "I have come to realize that touch can be a prayer that has a power all its own." Beautiful as that is I have since heard something more sublime. It does not surprise me to find saints describe God's intimate communion with them as the--Divine Touch.

STRESS

Since stress is a pre-onset condition to all disease, stress management becomes critical.

I'm going to stick my neck way out now and state my belief that stress is a pre-onset condition to all diseases. I purposefully didn't use a qualifier and say "most" or "many" diseases. I mean *all* diseases. Perhaps someone more knowledgeable than I could challenge my belief; however, no one has yet.

Most physicians now recognize and accept the fact that stress causes and/or accelerates between seventy and ninety percent of all medical complaints. The American Academy of Family Physicians states that two-thirds of all patients visiting family doctors are "driven" there by stress-related symptoms.

As a cancer patient, examining his history in great detail, looking for insight and understanding of how I might have contributed to my illness, I could see that stress and stress-management loomed very large. I concluded that I did not manage stress well at all. And, I added to this fact my belief that illness is never purely a physical problem: that there is a psychosomatic component that needs attention; that emotional and mental states play a most significant role in susceptibility to cancer and other diseases; and the oh-so-important message, that recovery from all disease requires better coping mechanisms.

It seems reasonable to me to assume that if we can get physiologically sick from responding psychologically to stress in some inappropriate way, we can perhaps get well by learning to control the psychological response.

The origin of psychosomatic disease seems to lie

in a person's *response to stress*. I find it easy to believe that physiological stress can destroy the body, changing biochemical functions or changing neural patterns. However, it's not generally understood that psychological stress also destroys the body in ways similar to physiological stress.

A section of the subcortex called the limbic system (also known as the "visceral" brain and sometimes referred to as the "emotional" brain) responds to emotions. First you have a thought, even if you're not aware of it, thoughts sometime going through us in milliseconds. Another way of stating this is that a thought always precedes an emotion.

This limbic response to emotions changes neurological firing patterns. Since the limbic system is connected by multiple pathways to various other structures, including the hypothalamus (the neural control center that regulates to a large extent the autonomic nervous system), emotional response is spread out into autonomic control centers and modifies ongoing autonomic functions. In the evolution of mankind this mechanism was clearly needed to respond to danger and to protect life and limb.

Most of you have read, or heard, accounts of how our ancestors faced natural dangers. From the dawn of human history people fought off and hunted life-threatening animals. Homo sapiens learned quickly when to "fight or take flight," or else they perished. When confronted with danger the body responds in several ways: the muscles tense, the heart pounds, breathing comes faster, adrenaline pours into your blood, your feet and hands become cold, your blood flow is restricted to the center of the body, etc. The dinosaur, bear, lion, saber-toothed tiger have been replaced by a modern "jungle." We are

now facing more pervasive threats/"killers"...the guy
blowing his horn at you because you are not driving
fast enough; (definition of a split second: time lapse
between traffic light turning green and guy behind
you blowing his horn); schedules and deadlines; income tax audits; bill collectors; college tuitions; air,
water and noise pollution; rising cost of living; threat
of nuclear disaster, and so on.
  Panic!
  Can I fight?
  Who?
  Do I run?
  Where?
  How? I tense up; my teeth grind; I break out in
a cold sweat. My body's engine is stuck in overdrive. The "engine" can't take that kind of wear and
tear too long. How do I cope? Take a drink? Reach
for the aspirin? Maybe the Maalox or Valium? There
has to be a better way! There are better coping
mechanisms. I'll cite some shortly.
  Caveman's response machinery follows this order:
        First you perceive/see something.
        Perception activates limbic area.
        Limbic or visceral section connects to
        hypothalamus.
        Hypothalamus controls autonomic (i.e.,
        supposedly involuntary functions) response.
  There is mounting evidence that six to eighteen
months (these are rough parameters) following a
stressful experience to one member of a family,
someone else will contract a degenerative disease.
Several of my physician friends have predicted very
accurately the onset of illness, following highly
stressful events in people's lives.
  In the early 1950's, University of Washington

gle common denominator for stress, even for an astronaut, is "the necessity of significant change in the life pattern of the individual." Holmes found that among tuberculosis patients, for example, the onset of the disease had generally followed a cluster of disruptive events: a death in the family, a new job, marriage. Stress did not cause the illness, Holmes emphasizes--"It takes a germ"--but tension did seem to promote the disease process. Holmes discovered that merely discussing upsetting events could produce physiological changes. An experiment in which sample biopsies were taken before and after discussions of certain subjects showed that "we caused tissue damage just by talking about a mother-in-law's coming to visit," say Holmes. The example, he notes, is not facetious: "A person often catches a cold when a mother-in-law comes to visit. Patients mentioned mother-in-law so often that we come to consider them a common cause of disease in the U.S."

I found an almost perfect correlation between stressful events in my life and outbreaks of cancer. This also fits my belief about "no coincidences in life."

In 1972 I was completing work on my doctoral thesis. When I went in for my oral defense I looked for some visual, nonverbal sign from one of my thesis committee members as to what I could expect. He looked sad and shook his head from side-to-side. My stomach hit the floor. I had difficulty breathing. I was told my thesis wasn't acceptable in its current form and they gave me three weeks to make necessary changes. I hired a secretary, and we worked ten to twelve hour days, seven days a week to complete the job, which was finally approved. Stressful--whewee!!

That same year I lost my job working with the Farmington, Connecticut school system in Project Empathy, a compensatory educational program for disadvantaged youngsters. The government funding had run out. The loss of the job was bad, but the negative effects caused by the termination were even more painful. My self-worth diminished. There was domestic pressure because my wife became the sole "breadwinner" in our family. We had to reduce our standard of living. Get the picture? Stressful? You bet!

June and I sold our "dream house" (because of the long commute), and moved to Longmeadow, Massachusetts. I started teaching at Springfield College, and June became the art director at Albert Steiger, Inc., a department store in Springfield. Stress points are accumulating! On of my brothers died from illness, and a cousin, a policeman, was shot to death. A few months later, another brother died of cancer. As you already know, on July 10, 1973, my first cancer surgery took place, a total laryngectomy:

One summer back in the 1960's I was directing Camp Winding Trails, a summer day camp in Farmington, Connecticut. A seven-year-old child drowned in the lake. I was devastated. The dead youngster's parents started a lawsuit. The pressure on me was more than flesh and blood could bear. A strange phenomenon occurred: my hair started falling from my head in large clumps. There's not a bald head in my family tree. Could it have been the stress? I think so. (My hair did grow back...just in case you were wondering).

Some studies have demonstrated that repressed anger may increase chances of breast cancer in women. An additional study showed that stress at critical times during pregnancies cause hormonal changes, adversely affecting unborn children. Another study showed that cervical cancer death rates are more than twice as high in divorced women as in married women.

Vietnam veterans experience significantly more cancers than non-veterans in the same age group. (These cancers were in addition to the ones caused by Agent Orange.)

The human brain hasn't changed in over 25,000 years. We are genetically programmed to "pull for pleasure and avoid pain." This holds up for me: it fits; it dovetails with my observations of clients' behaviors. When I confront them with the idea that they have choices and get payoffs from their behavior--as would be expected--they deny it. "You think I like this stuff going on in my life?" You see, even if what you are doing is painful, the alternative appears even more painful. Therefore, the pleasure-pain principle still applies. Remember when you were a teenager and you had fantasies about that cute boy or girl you wanted to date? Too many of us did what I did. I scared myself into inactivity by the fearful thought, "Suppose she tells me, 'buzz off you pimple faced creep?'" So I didn't dare risk the great pain of rejection, even though I was hurting to ask her for a date.

I got into a heated discussion one day with an older school principal who argued that youngsters today are under no greater pressure than when he was a child back in the 1920's and 1930's. I reminded this person our "kids" are privy to every disaster in the United States and throughout the rest of the world through modern communication methods and news media. Like me, I'm sure they're frustrated and feeling helpless at times because they do care and live in a world of uncertainties. That very week I sat in front of my television set watching a group of young people in the United States carry on a debate via satellite with some students in England. I was awe-struck by their worldly knowledge. (I want to make it clear, at this time, that I'm optimistic about the future. Our youngsters will figure out ways to repair the damage we adults caused).

The school principal and I were at cross-purposes for a number of years. I was working to keep youngsters in school, and he wanted to "push" them out. (Many so called "drop-outs" are more accurately "push-outs"). I still believe that modern civilization carries in its wake stress-created effects that we must learn to understand and control to maintain our sanity and good health.

I find it appalling, and a reflection of the times, that the three (3) top selling drugs in the United States are Valium the ubiquitous tranquilizer, Tagamet, an ulcer medication, and Inderal for hypertension. We have less to worry about from the Russians and some Third World nation than from the way we live. We'll kill ourselves from within faster than be killed from some foreign invader.

In my library research of stress-and-illness connections, I come across numerous studies, too many to mention at this time, where the consensus is that there is a relationship between major stressful events in a person's life and ill health. History provides multiple examples of this conclusion. The blitz of London, England in 1940-1941 showed significant increases in illness due to the distress of the bombing, and the illness rate continued to climb persistently throughout the bombing. The rate of illness returned to normal with the ending of the blitz in 1941. The same story happened in Athens, Greece, following an earthquake in 1981.

Another fascinating study showed that several family life changes occurred during the two years prior to the onset of leukemia in a child within that family.

Another study was done with identical twins, where only one of the twins died due to coronary artery disease. The researcher found significantly higher life-change events, prior to death, for the twin that dies than for the one who had survived.

Some experts believe stress is more the result of everyday, petty annoyances. I heard a priest one time say, "It's not the boulders in the road of life that stop us. It's the pebbles we get in our shoes." In terms of stress, the "pebbles" may be the everyday annoyances or "hassles" we allow to bother us: the cap that was left off the toothpaste; the family delinquent who forgot to take out the garbage; the sister who wore your blouse and didn't press and put it back on a hanger; the car stalling in traffic. Policeman find "soft" judges and ineffective judicial systems more stressful than a "breaking-and-entering" call. Human-helping professionals "burn out" more from being "paper pushers" and devalued professionals than from low pay. Teachers find it more stressful dealing with the "system" and irate parents than "hard-to-reach" students.

At a conference in 1979 entitled, "The Crisis in Stress Research: A Critical Reappraisal", the experts in attendance were in general agreement that there is a relationship between life stress and the onset of disease. The correlations, however, I must add in fairness, are not explanations. There is still much research needed in this vital area.

My suspicion is that personality traits and persistent negative emotions have a big part to play in cancer and in other diseases. These traits and feel-ings all too often appear in the cancer patients I counsel: hostility and resentment toward someone or something, rejection and frustration, hopelessness and depression, helplessness and anxiety.

Gerald Jampolski, M.D. says "THE FIRST STEP TO HAPPINESS IS FORGIVENESS." People need to learn to forgive real and imagined insults. Stop car-rying around this excess baggage that is self-devour-ing and energy-sapping. Approximately ten million Americans take five hundred billion minor tranquilizers each year. They think this is *the* way to deal with stressful activities. If there's one thing I learned from my "junkies", it's that when you con-tinue to take any drug, tolerance and toxicity go hand-in-hand. In other words, as you build up a tol-erance for the drug, you need to take larger doses to get the desired effect. At the same time your body is becoming more and more toxic. There are better ways of coping. I will briefly discuss some of these methods--enough, perhaps, to "put a burr under your saddle," to get you to seek techniques that work for you in stress reduction.

Many people I know I refer to as "adrenaline freaks." They seem to love the excitement of "brinksmanship." Are you one of those people who wait until the last minute and then "rush like hell" to catch the train, bus, or plane? Breathe a sigh of relief when you squeak in just seconds before the board of directors meeting begins? Enjoy Rus-sian roulette kinds of activities like motor bike rac-ing, skydiving, mountain climbing? Life in the fast lane. Wowee! Caution, you "freaks": you may be headed for danger.

None of us are going to escape this life without our share of trials and tribulations. We all have our dramas. The key to survival, as it appears to me, is how we deal with those tough times. Our coping behaviors make the difference. We must learn to cope, or we'll succumb.

For all of the major known causes of death in the United States, widows die at rates three to thirteen times as high as married women. It's not a coincidence. The contributing factors include such things as loss of a social support network (i.e., family and friends); a diminished sense of self-worth because they didn't establish an identity for themselves other than mother and housewife; a learned helplessness and hopelessness; and a feeling of isolation.

I offer the following holistic suggestions to cope with stress. Some are common sense; others, not easily perceived. All together they nourish and detoxify, strengthen and relax the body, renew your mind, and refresh and recharge your spirit.

How To Cope With Stress

1. Quit smoking.
2. Lose weight, if necessary.
3. Modify your diet, cutting down on sugar, salt, and caffeine, increasing your B complex intake as part of your nutritional supplements of vitamins and minerals, cutting out fatty foods.
4. Do some reading in Cognitive Therapy. We can all improve our irrational thought processes, the automatic negativities which cause stress.
5. Get a good exercise program started, after a physical checkup by your physician. *Keep the exercise fun.*
6. Get some training in relaxation techniques. I have no favorite here: Transcendental

Meditation (TM), self-hypnosis, biofeedback, yoga, directed daydreaming, guided imagery, and others. There are contraindicators for some of these methods. Check with your doctor. No single approach to relaxation is right for everyone.

7. Take periodic breaks/vacations/time-out.
8. Eliminate some of the "everyday," petty annoyances (the pebbles in your shoe).

You need a complete program to deal with distress. Relaxation techniques will not rid your body of the toxic substances you've accumulated. Exercise will not help if you continue to eat poorly, smoke, and drink alcohol in excessive amounts. It's important that you understand this. "Play with a full deck." There are no gurus, no magic bullets! Get back in control of your life. You don't have to be a victim of your body or your environment.

From my limited knowledge, one of the body's fastest reactions when we are experiencing distress is that bile is ejected from the gall bladder into the small intestines (the upper part) and used to digest fats. Without bile, fats cannot be digested. Under stress, bile content is *reduced* almost instantaneously, allowing the free Fatty Acid (FFA) count to increase to injurious levels. Needless to say, fatty foods are to be avoided during stressful times in particular, and generally speaking as well.

Most people under stressful conditions experience acid indigestion or react with diarrhea or constipation. Many laboratory experiments have proved conclusively that your digestive organs can be adversely affected by stress. Stress makes heavy demands on our metabolism. Our digestive organs may become over-stimulated or suppressed.

Experiments have been done where Heparin

locks (intravenous blood sampling units) were inserted in the arm of each family member. As family members felt supported or excluded, FFA levels were calculated. As each person experienced more stress, the FFA count increased. As they felt their own anxiety levels decreased, so did the FFA count.

Tension/distress comes to all sensitive people. If you are faced with the loss of a loved one, loss of status, loss of anything you value, you become distressed. The tensions that occur physiologically may retard circulation and prevent any organ in your body from getting its proper nourishment. The result? Illness, disease, breakdown, cancer can generate anywhere in your body.

The number of T-cells, of T-lymphocytes, that our bodies produce to destroy mutant cells that create tumors is reduced when we are stressed. Chronic stress suppresses the immune system, the response which normally prevents the multiplication of these cells, and the cells grow crazily, out of control.

Another way of saying this is that T-cells are decreased during stress responses and increased when we relax. Some people still think this belief is controversial. You decide for yourself.

Don't wait until you get cancer to learn the habits of good health. Most of the health problems that exist in modern American society are not caused by the infectious diseases that killed millions of people only a few decades ago. Stress allowed to become distress, is one, if not the biggest, reason modern populations are experiencing epidemic proportions of cancer, heart attack, stroke, arthritis. Mechanized medicine and the use of drugs will not prevent these contemporary illnesses. You are the one to prevent these maladies from afflicting you and your loved ones.

The goal of stress management is not to eliminate all stress. That's an impossibility, as long as you're alive. Besides, there are two kinds of stress: Joyful stress, known as eustress, such as winning a prize, getting a job promotion and bad stress, called distress. Life would be very dull without both kinds of stress. Somehow we must learn to limit the harmful effects of stress, without going to an extreme and living a boring life devoid of challenge and vitality. Find out the optimal amount of stress you can tolerate and stay healthy. Get the most out of life with the least amount of strain.

For the purpose of reinforcement, I repeat: You and I must accept and understand that we have more control over our bodies than we ever realized. More often than not, we allow ourselves to become ill. We can stop seeing ourselves as helpless victims of fate and sickness. We have the ability to prevent almost all illnesses and diseases.

I believe that both the prevention and treatment of cancer must incorporate a stress-management program, carefully planned out and zealously carried out. Do some careful thinking and planning about your stress-management program--and begin *NOW*.

HOW I FEEL NOW

PART FOUR

AM I BETTER?

I am no longer wasting my life, and I often feel as if I've found the Fountain of Youth. I sense a tremendous rebirth.

Partly because I've said, and believe, that in many ways I'm better for having had cancer and partly because some members of the medical community refer to me as the "miracle man", literally dozens of cancer patients have contacted me to help them. I make it very clear to them that I don't have *the* answer. I am not privy to any exotic lotions or potions or notions. I haven't received any tablets from a Higher Source, nor have I had any supernatural revelations. There is no escape from reality.

My response to their need is to get these patients to dig into themselves and to find the bodily and mental controls that will enable them to live *consciously* and *deliberately* and, therefore, more fruitfully. I urge those who seek my counsel not to abandon traditional medicine but to be sure to incorporate a holistic approach into their treatment. Find your own juices and use your own gray matter. Concoct your own conscious worry-free lifestyle that brings you a kind of peace and contentment. In other words, I invite them to grow. Sounds utopian? It may be. But I just have this conviction that lives can be better-lived.

Once I heard the renowned Elisabeth Kubler-Ross say that maybe the world will not be better off if a cancer cure is found. This sounded strange to my ears. I heard it and couldn't (or wouldn't) internalize it at that time. Reflecting on what she said, I've begun to think I know what she meant. The beautiful growth experienced to many cancer patients and

159

their kin would be lost.   Cancer provided those
wonderful opportunities to achieve all kinds of
growth--intellectual, emotional, and spiritual.   And I
can testify that I have seen all three kinds of growth
in my own life.

One of my favorite mentors used to say, "Ray, in
counselling clients, you only go as far as your insecu-
rities will permit you."   I'm much more secure now
than ever before and still growing, both professionally and personally.   "Watch out you anchor drag-
gers; move over because I'm going by!"   This teacher also used to say, "Your clients will never be
'weller' than you are, so continue to grow."   Let me
state here and now that I'm also "weller" than I've
ever been before in my life.   And all of that is due to
the growing I've done since my first diagnosis of
cancer.

I have grown intellectually.   In addition to acquir-
ing a broader base of knowledge, I have evaluated
my goals in life.   I know that personal success has
little to do with childish fantasies, with adolescent
dreams of glitz and glamour, and with immature adult
goals of power and privilege.   Instead, labor and love
are what it's all about.   Earl Nightingale, wrote
"...success comes to the person who knows what's
important and what isn't.   The unsuccessful person
always has them mixed up: he puts the unimportant
ahead of the important and grows small and bitter,
disillusioned and scared.   We will find successful
people in all walks of life, in all income brackets.   To
succeed is to do something very well--whatever it is--
and to have someone to love who returns that love."

Often we sacrifice too much for tinsel and trifles,
the fleeting, temporary values our neighbor and society holds up as symbols of success.   I heard a
wonderful story about Benjamin Franklin when he

was a seven-year-old boy. I don't know whether or not the story is true, but the moral is what grabs me. On Ben's seventh birthday his family gave him a pocketful of coins so he could go into town and buy his own gift. Ben met another young boy, "street wise" and a little older, playing with a whistle. Ben wanted the whistle and was soon charmed out of all his money in exchange for that whistle. Ben returned home with his new, prized possession and told his brothers and sisters how lucky he was. They all had a good laugh and pointed out to Ben that he had paid way too much for a very cheap whistle.

Years later Ben would often say in observing the choices and practices of associates, friends, and family members, "You're paying too much for that whistle," The point, obviously, is that we all are guilty sometimes of paying a "price" far in excess of the worth of the "prize." A few examples. As an educator I'm appalled at: efforts to teach one- and two-year-old children to read; "teachers" who act like Gestapo in some private enterprise teaching centers, shouting and screaming at children, holding a child's face in a vice-like grip to force the child to focus on the blackboard; parents who beat and starve their children for some misdemeanor or imagined insult; conditional love and protection for children; a current governmental belief that a larger defense budget is more important than health, education, and rehabilitation services. We do pay too much for our "whistles."

The area of greatest growth for me has been emotional. These days I am aware of my feelings. I acknowledge them all honestly. I have learned that it is our ideas about ourselves, about events, about life that trigger our feelings. So I cultivate constructive thoughts, encourage positive feeling, and communicate my pain and my appreciation. I know I can influence my attitudes and accept full responsibility for my feeling. I'm convinced others are capable of doing the same. I've acquired more positive beliefs, and I've gained the knowledge that I can change almost anything about myself. You can, too.

What you feel depends on how you see things. That's illustrated by a wonderful scene in the musical *Milk and Honey*. Here two different individuals perceive and experience the same thing. But the feelings are diametrically opposite. The scene takes place in the early settlement of Israel.

One character sings:

This is the land of milk and honey.
This is the land of sun and song.
This is the world of good and plenty.
Humble and proud and young and
strong.
This is the land that heaven blessed,
And this lovely land is mine.

The second person counters with this version:

The honey's kind of bitter and milk's a
little sour.
Do you know the pebble is the State's
official flower?
How about the tensions,
Political dissensions, and
No one ever mentions that the scenery
is barren,
and torrid and arid and horrid, and
How about the border when the
Syrians attack?
How about the Arabs with a rifle at
your back?

How about the water, etc.

We can invoke positive or negative feelings not only about a place,but we can also do the same with ourselves. The loss of my body's integrity was a sad and angry experience. It also became an opportunity to risk and to grow and to develop more positive attitudes about myself--that it was O.K. and desirable to take good care of myself and to strive for high-level wellness. I don't want, nor do I need, the pay-offs that come with illness. My needs and wants are O.K. and deserve to be met. I'll find the time in health to be with my family; to have "play-time" with my wife and friends; to listen to my music; to give up the neurotic pursuit of perfection; to stop being driven to "hurry up," to "be strong," and to "try harder;" to never negotiate or deny any of my feelings; to accept to a greater degree than I ever appreciated before that I am the captain of my fate.

It is disheartening to see people who continue self-destructive behavior/practices/habits. It is evident that they don't love themselves enough. Would you knowingly allow a child to engage in self-destructive activities? Of course not. You care too much for that child and want to prevent injury. Why should it be less for yourself? Don't you love yourself enough to stop? It really is disturbing to me to see cancer patients continue to smoke, drink, and eat poorly.

Most of us get little education about our emotions and about communication skills. During the 1960's I attended all kinds of encounter-groups and went to numerous sensitivity training programs; and like hundreds of thousands of people during that generation, I discovered layers of tape wrapped around my emotions and intuitions that needed to be penetrated, like a festering boil that needs lancing. I have a greater willingness now to confront openly and honestly all feelings, all thoughts, all experiences. The level of communication opened during my cancer battle has led to a greater degree of closeness and depth in my relationships with my wife, my family, my friends, my students.

In contrast to this, I find people at large do not communicate. Children and parents don't understand each other. Employers complain, "Those people down there don't listen to us." Teachers complain about students and students about teachers: "They don't listen to us." Husbands and wives--forget it! It takes twenty years of marriage to finally communicate with one another--if it ever happens. There are too many lives lived in little, compartmentalized worlds, too terrified to risk contact. What a terrible loss.

Then, there is the communication that reduces and demeans people, detraction at its worse. This happens with cancer patients. Cancer is such a pervasive, dreaded disease that when others discover you are a cancer patient, your cancer becomes your identity. Some students who haven't had a course with me refer to me as "the prof with throat cancer." My cancer becomes my defining characteristic.

While I was a patient in a cancer clinic I became frustrated, at one point, with the nature of repeated encounters with other cancer patients and their families. With them, the conversations and questions were incessantly about cancer. I got on the telephone with June and said, "Sweetheart, who the hell am I?"

June asked for clarification because she didn't understand the intent of the question. I explained my anger at being solely identified as a cancer patient. "Please tell me...I need reminders of my many other roles in life." She proceeded to enumerate: "You're my husband, friend, lover; father to our children; teacher, counsellor, consumer, advocate, charmer, brother, son, etc. You are you! Damned right I am. I am somebody in all my complexities and in all my varied roles. *Incidentally,* I have cancer.

My wife and I know the pain that comes when we fail to communicate our appreciation. We are much more apt to communicate our dissatisfaction than our gratitude. When my mother-in-law died suddenly from a cerebral hemorrhage, the most painful aspect for my wife to deal with was the fact that she didn't have time to tell her mother how much she loved and appreciated her. This "unfinished business" rested very heavily on June's conscience until several months later she had a therapy session with our dear friend, John Miller. He allowed June to go through the catharsis of her mother's death, but not before telling her mother all the sweet thoughts she carried around in her heart. The experience was now a completion, a Gestalt, and June is much relieved.

I had a similar experience when my brother Lou died of cancer. I visited him weeks and months before he died and thought to myself, "You are such a beautiful man, Lou. Do you realize how much you are loved and will be missed when you depart this life?" *I never said it to him.* I sat on the edge of his bed and held his hand when the end came, but he was too delirious to hear me. I want to believe he heard my unspoken thoughts. It would have been so much better, however, had I told him my feelings--better for the two of us. (By the way, he was moved to what appeared to me to be a "utility clos-

et" at the end of the hall, where he could be avoided...and die alone.)

I no longer carry around this excess baggage of
"unfinished business." I express my love and appreciation. I'll never get caught short again, holding
back. Those moments are too precious, too fleeting.

Even "negative" emotions can have positive spin-
offs. Elisabeth Kubler-Ross said we treat the emotions of grief and pain in life as something bad but
that these experiences are really gifts.

When you look back at the anguish, suffering and
traumas in your life, you'll see that these are periods
of biggest growth. After a loss that brings you
dreadfully painful months, you are a different man, a
different woman. Of course, you can't tell parents
who have just lost a child that they will see the event
as a growth experience. But many years later, they
will be able to look back and see the positive things-
-togetherness in their family, faith, or whatever--that
came out of their pain.

Spiritually I am still growing. I see an intercon-
nectedness to life, underlying the mystery. For me,
life itself, the daily unfolding, is high adventure. I am
present to whatever comes, living fully in the moment.

One of the most influential men in my life--a
wonderful role model--was a beautiful, smiling Irish-
man named Mark Moran, one of the early pioneers
in the Boys' Club movement. I spent countless
hours with the man at the Springfield Boys' Club and
the Boys' Club Summer Camp in Brimfield, Massachusetts. "Uncle" Mark had more maxims and
rules for living than anyone I have ever met, quick,
short lessons that stuck in my mind. I remember
them all. The following are just a few that I cata-

logued:

- 'Tis better to build a fence on the cliff than an ambulance down in the valley.
- A man never stands so straight and tall as when he stoops to help a child.
- It's not the size of the dog in the fight that counts. It's the size of the fight in the dog that does.
- A mystery is a truth which we do not fully understand.

The last one is my favorite.

In my search for answers, for missing truths, in the mystery of my cancer fight I learned a great deal and am still mystified by much. As I did, you must find your own way. Cull from what I've shared with you but follow your own instincts. Be your own guru. Give love. Be open to what is possible and contributes to abundant living. Be willing at the very least to listen, to read, to contemplate what once appeared as exotic and esoteric. I'm thinking about subjects like acupuncture, psychic healing, the laying on of hands, solar influences, telepathy, and others. Don't be finished *before* you die. Continue to risk, to communicate, and to grow. Have passionate desires. Think that there are more discoveries for you. I expect to exit this world "kicking" because there are still more things I want to experience.

Dr. Bernard Siegel, founder and director of a program in New Haven, Connecticut, called ECAP (Exceptional Cancer Patients), distributes bumper stickers that read "Anticipate Miracles." I do. I also find it beneficial to be not too much of a realist. I've become an optimist, an important attribute in all human-helping professionals.

Elisabeth Kubler-Ross says the greatest lesson she

and her students and patients learned is this: LIVE,
so you do not have to look back and say: God, how
I have wasted my life."

I'm no longer wasting my life, and I often feel
like I've found the Fountain of Youth. I sense a
tremendous rebirth, like the lead character in *Milk
and Honey* when he sings:

> Like a young man,
> With a young dream,
> You will hear me laughing at time.
> I will plow the desert in the morning
> With the power of a boy,
> Guard the border if I have to; in the blare of
> the sun
> I can handle a gun like a toy.
> I'll make rainbows out of nowhere,
> 'Til the gray skies turn into gold,
> Like a young man who's young forever,
> I'll swear I'll never grow old.

Let me describe a mundane experience that re-
flects the more vital me, fully present to the moment. One day I met June for lunch. It was a cool,
rainy day in the greater Springfield, Massachusetts,
area. "Where would you like to go," I asked. She
replied, "How about something real fancy--an epi-
curean feast? Let's go to the White Hut."

The White Hut is a restaurant located in West
Springfield, Massachusetts, that serves sensational hot
dogs and hamburgers. They taste great in any
weather, but on a rainy day a lot of the natives had
the same idea June had. The place was packed
three-deep at the counter. Lots of familiar faces; lot
of noise; lots of laughter. Busy, busy place. Hur-
ried, yet not strained. A comfortable, at-home

feeling. The ambience is terrific. The sights, sounds, and aromas are familiar. If you want service, you have to shout. If you don't yell, you don't get taken care of. Make your wants known. No shyness permitted.

A red, white, and blue Volkswagen with large printed letters on the sides reading "WILBRAHAM BARBER SHOP" pulls into the parking lot. The driver gets out and thunders for all to hear, "How can I get to the world-famous Wilbraham Barber Shop?" Everyone gets a good laugh because they're all in on the joke.

The working staff behind the counter moves with great efficiency. All jobs are interchangeable. One person loads the grill, moves over to the cash register, and a second person fills in at the grill. A third person serves coffee and leaves to get some napkins. Without missing a beat someone else picks up the coffee pot and carries on. The choreography would do Gene Kelly proud.

I observed so much. I was aware of so much going on around me. This tiny restaurant, frequented by the wealthy and the poor, businessmen in three-piece suits, truck drivers, teachers, auto mechanics, and so on. A wonderful microcosm of life. People knowing and accepting the ground rules. Cooperating to make the place work. Simple, basic life in harmony. Pre-cancer I never would have taken in so much information or been so involved. Nor would I have found so much pleasure in such a simple activity. It's wonderful to be awake and alive.

Ernest Hemingway, in *For Whom the Bell Tolls*, says, "Ask not for whom the bell tolls. It tolls for thee." John Steinbeck's character Jody, in the *Grapes of Wrath*, speaks of a universal soul. What are these authors, and others, saying to us? I think they are saying that at some cosmological level we are all connected. When I read about starving children all over the world, it hurts me. I feel for the Sikhs in India being persecuted for the fanatics who assassinated Indira Gandhi. I cried profusely for Martin Luther King, Robert Kennedy, and John Kennedy. I feel related to the coolie I see in a photograph, tired and hungry, in China, resting after pulling his rickshaw. I like myself more for these feelings. It's not heroic to want to do good, to be compassionate, and, hopefully, to understand. It's mature. I am an appreciator. I've learned to care. I want to communicate that caring.

Some readers will find me too facile and too optimistic about life and about what human beings can achieve. Without apology I confess that I am an optimist, and I do believe that God wants us to be co-creators of an increased personal and social harmony on earth.

When I was in the United States Army, back in the 1950's, I was the Director of American Youth Activities in Southern Germany. One day I took a group of teenagers on a camping trip in the Black Forest. I went to get some supplies on my own and started hiking through the forest. I saw a sight that was absolutely awesome. A man who reminded me of Charlton Heston's Moses coming off the mountain was walking the same trail I was. He was over six feet tall, with a full head and beard of snow-white hair. "Majestic" fails to capture the essence, the presence of this fantastic figure of a man. He smiled, and we greeted one another and proceeded to hike together in long silences. Every so often he would point out some especially interesting natural phenomenon. He drew me into "his" enchanted world of nature. There were numerous times when he would ask me, "Did you see that shy creature peeking at us from the hollow of that tree?" I had to admit I missed the opportunity. We continued on in silence, and he would suddenly ask, "Did you notice that beautiful bird?" Repeatedly I was embarrassed that I had missed scenes of beauty all around me. At the same time, I was inspired by his awareness and knowledge. In transactional analysis terms, he saw the forest through a child's wondering eyes. Finally, at one point, he asked, "Did you see that black squirrel?" And when I turned to ask, "Where," he replied, "Too late." And gently, oh so gently, chided me with, "You miss so much."

Not any more. I take in all sorts of information with the receptors of my body. I'm also extremely sensitive to the needs of all living things in my environment. Almost daily, I witness "tiny" miracles of nature around me. I feel at one with all living species. I'm awestruck by the mysteries of life. I wish (naively, of course) that we would stop killing our animals, except when absolutely necessary. I find it hard to accept the fact that so many Americans fail to perceive the sacredness of life and fail to reverence all living things.

The following poem by Fyodor Dostoyevsky explains far better than I what I experience in my new affinity for all living things and in my renewed passion for life.

If you love everything, you will perceive the
divine mystery in things.
Once you perceive it, you will begin to
comprehend it better every day.
And you will come at last to love the whole world
with an all-embracing love.

NOTES

CHAPTER 1   pgs. 9, 10 - Elisabeth Kubler-Ross.
pg. 13 - Lyrics of Song "Welcome Home" from musical, FANNY, words and music by Harold Rome.

CHAPTER 2   pgs. 19-22 - Dr. Charlene DeLoach and Dr. Robert Greer, Adjustment to Severe Physical Disability.

CHAPTER 3   pg. 30 - Elisabeth Kubler-Ross, Death, The Final Stage of Growth.

CHAPTER 5   pg. 35 - Thomas Aquinas, "Miracles Are Simply Undiscovered Knowledge."
pg. 36 - Claudius Galenus, "Today's Radicalism   Becomes Tomorrow's Orthodoxy."
pg. 36 - Professor Richard Ahreus.
pg. 37 - Dr. John Diamond.
pg. 38 - Arthur C. Clark "Third Law."
pg. 39 - Professor Anna Aslan.

CHAPTER 6   pg. 43 - Elisabeth Kubler-Ross.
pg. 45 - Lyrics of song, "I Like You," from musical, FANNY.

CHAPTER 7   pg. 51 - Orville Kelley, "Make Today Count."
pg. 51-53 - Dr. Norman Vincent Peale, An Exciting Day Everyday.
pg. 55. - Lyrics of song, "Let's Not Waste A Moment," from musical, Milk and Honey, words and lyrics by Jerry Herman.
pg. 57 - Ernest Becker, The Denial of Death.
pg. 58 - Lawrence LeShan, The Mechanic and The Gardener.
pg. 63 - Poem by Richard Allen, in book by Elisabeth Kubler-Ross.

CHAPTER 8   pgs. 67-80 - Hedges Caper and Tabbie Kailer International Transactional Analysis Journals.

CHAPTER 10   pg. 94 - Porter Shimer, Fitness Through Pleasure.

pg. 98 - Dr. Szent Gyorbyi, Executive Health.

pg. 98, 99 - Publisher's Forward, Toxemia Explained by J. H. Tilden, M.D.

pg. 99 - Dr. Henry G. Bieler, Food Is Your Best Medicine.

CHAPTER 11   pg. 105 - Dr. Charles Moertel, New England Journal of Medicine.

pg. 107 - Professor Benjamin V. Siegel.

pg. 108 - Doctors Linus Pauling and Ewan Cameron.

CHAPTER 12   pg. 113 - Dr. Richard A. Passwater, Selenium As Food And Medicine.

CHAPTER 13   pg. 123 - O. Carl Simonton, Getting Well Again.

CHAPTER 14   pgs. 127-129 - Dr. John Diamond, Your Body Doesn't Lie.

pg. 132 - John N. Ott, Health and Light

CHAPTER 15   pg. 137 - Lyrics to song, "Love Is A Very Light Thing," from musical, FANNY.

pg. 138 - Dr. Hans Manksch, in Elisabeth Kubler-Ross' book, Death, The Final Stage of Growth.

pg. 140 - American Journal of Nursing, 1970, Dr. Dolores Krieger.

CHAPTER 16   pg. 151 - Jerry Jampols

CHAPTER 17   pg. 159 - Elisabeth Kubler-Ross.

pg. 160 - Earl Nightingale.

pg. 162 - Title song lyrics from musical, Milk and Honey.

pg. 166 - Elisabeth Kubler-Ross.

pg. 168 - Lyrics to song, "Like A Young Man," from musical, Milk and Honey.

pg. 171 - Poem by Fyodor Dostoyevsky.

BIBLIOGRAPHY

Benson, M.D., Herbert. *The Mind/Body Effect.*
New York, N. Y. A Berkley Book. 1979.
181 pages.

Bieler, M.D., Henry G. *Food is Your Best Medicine.*
New York, N.Y. Vintage Books. 1965. 236 pages.

Briggs, Dorothy Corkille. *Celebrate Yourself.*
Garden City, N.Y. Doubleday & Co., Inc. 1977.
226 pages.

Burns, M.D., David D. *Feeling Good.* New York,
N.Y. Signet Books. 1980. 416 pages.

Chopra, M.D., Deepak. *Creating Health, Beyond
Prevention, Toward Perfection.* Boston, Mass.
Houghton Mifflin Co. 1987. 224 pages.

Colton, Helen. *Touch Therapy.* New York, N.Y.
Kensington Publishing Corp. Copyright 1983.
Reprinted by arrangement with G. P. Putnam's
Sons. 314 pages.

Davis, Adelle. *Let's Get Well.* New York, N.Y. Signet
Books from New American Library. Copyright
1965 by Harcourt Brace Jovanovich, Inc. 476
pages.

DeLoach, Charlene and Greer, Bobby G. *Adjustment
To Severe Physical Disability.* New York, N.Y.
McGraw-Hill, Inc. 1981. 310 pages.

Diamond, M.D., John. *Your Body Doesn't Lie.* New
York, N.Y. Warner Books. 1980. 208 pages.

Emery, Gary. *Own Your Own Life.* New York, N.Y.
Signet Books. 1982. 331 pages.

Emery, Stewart. *The Owner's Manual For Your Life.*
New York, N.Y. Pocket Books. 1982. 224 pages.

Hendin, David. *Death As A Fact of Life*. New York,
N.Y. Warner Paperback Library. Published by
arrangement with W. W. Norton & Co., Inc.
1974. 223 pages.

Hutschnecker, M.D., Arnold A. *The Will To Live*.
New York, N.Y Cornerstone Library. 1951.
190 pages.

Kubler-Ross, Elisabeth. *To Live Until We Say Good-
Bye*. Englewood Cliffs, N.J. Prentice-Hall, Inc.
1978. 160 pages.

_____. *Questions and Answers on Death and
Dying*. New York, N.Y. Macmillan Publishing
Co., Inc. 1974. 177 pages.

_____. *Death, The Final Stage of Growth*.
Englewood Cliffs, New Jersey. Prentice-Hall,
Inc. 181 pages.

LeShan, Lawrence. *The Mechanic and the Gardener*.
New York, N.Y. Holt, Rinehart and Winston.
1982. 217 pages

Lingerman, Hal A. *The Healing Energies of Music*.
Wheaton, Illinois. The Theosophical Publishing
House. 1983. 199 pages.

Miller, Don Ethan. *Bodymind, The Whole Person
Health Book* .York, N.Y. Pinnacle Books, Inc.
1974. 217 pages.

Newbold, M.D., H. L. *Vitamin C Against Cancer*.
Briarcliff Manor, New York. 1979. 363 pages.

Ott, John N. *Health and Light*. New York, N.Y.
Pocket Books. 1976. 222 pages.

Passwater, Richard A. *Selenium as Food & Medicine* .
New Canaan, Conn. Keats Publishing. 1980. 240
pages.
____.*Super-Nutrition*. New York, N.Y. Pocket
Books. 1975. 275 pages.
Pelletier, Kenneth R. *Holistic Medicine, From Stress
to Optimum Health.* New York, N.Y. Delacorte
Press/Seymour LLawrence. 1979. 330 pages.
___. *Mind As Healer. Mind As Slayer.* New York,
N.Y. Dell Publishing Co. 1977. 36 pages.

Regush, Nicholas M.. Editor. *Frontiers of Healing:
New* Dimensions in Parapsychology. New York,
N.Y. Avon Books. 1977. 309 pages.

Shimer, Porter. *Fitness Through Pleasure.* Emmaus,
PA. Rodale Press. 1982. 250 pages. Simonton,
M.D., O. Carl. *Getting Well Again.* New York,
N.Y. Bantam Books, Inc. 1978. 245 pages.
Stroebel, M.D., Charles F. *QR The Quieting Reflex.*
New York, N.Y. Berkley Books, published by
arrangement with G. P.

Tilden, M.D., J. H. *Toxemia Explained.* New
Canaan, Conn. Keats Publishing, Inc. 1976.
144 pages.

Weber, Barbara Ray. *The Reiki Factor.* Smithtown,
N.Y. Exposition Press. 1983. 142 pages.

DEDICATION & ACKNOWLEDGEMENT

I dedicate this book with love and gratitude to Alex Rossmann, who helped save my life. He taught, provoked, and inspired me. He is responsible for many of the ideas in this book. I welcome the opportunity to publicly thank him for the knowledge, caring, and refreshing breath of vitality he gave me when everything appeared hopeless.

Special Thanks

To Josephine Giorgi, a life-long friend, who spent countless hours editing and organizing my manuscript to the point where she could almost repeat it verbatim by memory.

To one of the best friends anyone ever had: Al Alissi. Your encouragement and emotional support were so vital to me. I can't thank you enough.

For my children, Jennifer and Keith, and especially my wife, June, who gave me support, encouragement, and understanding during my years of writing this book.

Postscript

In the midst of my fight for survival, I lost sight of the fact the significant others in my life were all struggling with, their own adjustments to my cancer.

After I completed my manuscript and it was going to press, my wife suggested that sometime soon I address more deeply and insightfully the issues faced by those who must "stand and wait" like the line from Milton's poem, "He also serves who only stands and waits."

There were numerous occasions when well intentioned people would ask about my well-being to express their concerns for me. June became painfully aware that her feelings and our children's fears were being discounted (i.e., treated like they didn't exist). I was too enmeshed in my own fears to hear her pleadings. I had figuratively died several times and she felt forced to mourn her sense of loss by herself. The psyche or spirit can't take too much of that kind of treatment. The isolation she experienced leads me to believe I need to address these issues in more depth in a future book.

There were non-verbal and behavioral indicators I missed, such as faces that looked sullen, blank or sad; voices which were either harsh and strident, or barely audible. The family's reason for being is the welfare of its individual members. This virtue got carried to an extreme and became a fault. My needs were so great, her needs were lost. I'm convinced an objective, professional counselor is needed by most families facing such traumas.

I'm pleased to share with you that there are nurturing things you can do; it is possible to create a spirit of involvement and mutual support for all family members; strategies that can be used to help families communicate better what is difficult for some members to express. But, I'm getting ahead of myself.

('Till next time . . .)